Leadership Wise

Why Business Books Suck, but Wise Leaders Succeed

Leadership Wise

Why Business Books Suck, but Wise Leaders Succeed

John W. Foreman

WILEY

Published by John Wiley & Sons, Inc., Hoboken, New Jersey.
Published simultaneously in Canada and the United Kingdom.

ISBNs: 9781394191680 (hardback), 9781394191697 (epdf), 9781394191703 (epub)

For general information on our other products and services or for technical support, please contact our Customer Care Department within the United States at (800) 762-2974, outside the United States at (317) 572-3993 or fax (317) 572-4002.

If you believe you've found a mistake in this book, please bring it to our attention by emailing our reader support team at wileysupport@wiley.com with the subject line "Possible Book Errata Submission."

Wiley also publishes its books in a variety of electronic formats. Some content that appears in print may not be available in electronic formats. For more information about Wiley products, visit our web site at www.wiley.com.

Library of Congress Control Number: 2023941189

Cover images: Papyrus: © MarekPhotoDesign.com/Adobe Stock, Portrait: © Olena/Adobe Stock
Cover design: Wiley

SKY10051046_071223

Contents at a Glance

Contents

Contents

Conclusion   *189*

Acknowledgments   *195*

About the Author   *197*

Index   *199*

To Lydia Foreman, who taught me about Wisdom Literature and gave me the idea for this book. I couldn't ask for a better wife and friend.

A Few Things Up Front

Hi! I'm John. I work as the chief product officer (CPO) at one of those tech unicorns you're always reading about called Podium. As far as unicorns go, we're pretty grounded. We're based in Utah, not Silicon Valley. Better skiing, worse cocktails.

We build software to help local businesses run their front office: things such as finding leads, talking with customers, collecting payment, marketing, and getting feedback. I'm in charge of making sure we build the *right* software. I'm paid to make good decisions (that's important. . .we'll get to that).

At Podium, we do regular training for all our managers. We found that oftentimes when things went awry, it wasn't a problem with the folks on the ground. No, they were often just "following orders." But somewhere in that managerial chain of the telephone game, things had gotten wonky. And while our managers were super smart, hardworking folks, many of them hadn't managed before, and they just needed some help being more effective. Hence, we implemented regular manager training. I was on board!

That is, I was on board until someone from HR asked me to conduct one of the training sessions.

"What do I talk about?" I asked.

"Whatever you want," they said, "perhaps your management philosophy or something topical to our values or what's going on in the business."

I replayed in my head things I'd heard in previous manager trainings. There had been content on managing your time wisely. There'd been a bit on holding folks accountable. I remember one leader shouting, "Fuck hustle culture!" All the people who'd presented their bits seemed to know what they were talking about. They had a perspective on work.

And then there was me.

"Uh, let me think about it and get back to you," I said.

Did I have anything to say about management? I'd been leading people since my first year out of grad school, and here I was with a graying beard, three kids, two dogs, a 20-year marriage, and absolutely zero to say about leadership. Well, not exactly zero. I had precisely two words to say.

It wasn't that I didn't think about leading. I thought about it constantly. I had to lead people every day! No, it was that every time I tried to distill my views on the topic, all that was left in the distillation was a 150-proof bottle of "it depends."

It depends. My leadership philosophy could be summarized in two words.

Shit. How was I going to train my managers in the subtle art of "it depends?" I started talking it through with my wife, Lydia. She doesn't work in tech like I do. No, she's got an academic background in Hebrew Bible and has spent much of her working life in ministry. When I told her that my leadership philosophy was "it depends," she understood me. She'd encountered it before in cultures that existed rather far away in space and time. She was able to give me some historical footholds for what felt like me just hanging off the side of a cliff all alone.

So I got to work trying to articulate just what I meant. I didn't have anything shocking to say like, "Fuck hustle culture!" I kinda like hustling. I also like naps. But I was able to clarify my milquetoast "it depends" philosophy.

I presented my thoughts to Podium's managers, and interestingly enough, they liked what I had to say! They agreed! I was shocked. Perhaps they were just sucking up? I hope not.

What follows in this book is my theory on leadership. There's not much to it, honestly. And what there is, well, I didn't make up. It's ancient. Dare I say, it's wisdom! But before we dive in, let's define our terms a bit.

Other Than Being a Bad Corporate Trainer, What Are My Qualifications?

It was a cold fall day in 2018. I had gotten out of bed in Atlanta, Georgia, with the gurgles. My stomach felt like a milkshake that someone was blowing bubbles into through a boba tea straw. Audibly so. I spent the morning gripping the sides of the toilet like a kid doing cannonballs at the pool. You get it. You've been there.

But today was an important day! Many of the product teams at Mailchimp (this is where I worked before Podium) had "showcase" meetings where they'd take myself (the CPO) and the chief technical officer through what they were working on. It was my chance to micromanage the hell out of them. Ooooooh, I lived for a good round of micromanagement. After I got off the toilet for the third time, I told Lydia I was going make a run for it. I grabbed a coconut LaCroix and headed out the door.

Now, Atlanta isn't known for its speedy commutes. I lived 7 miles from the Mailchimp office at the time, but that usually took me 25 minutes to drive. And even with a degree in mathematics, I hadn't done the math on the time between my intestinal "contractions."

I made it 10 minutes into my commute before I shit my pants. I remember the exact spot. It was here.

Source: John Foreman

I hit a U-turn faster than a mobster trying to lose a tail, stuffed my jacket between me and the seat, and gunned it home like Ryan Gosling in *Drive*; only my outfit was far less pearly white. I was 34 years old at the time.

I've never had a coconut LaCroix again. I never told that story to my colleagues at Mailchimp. *And I never again tried to push through the trots to make a meeting.*

This story is basically my entire professional life in a nutshell. I care deeply about my work. Perhaps a little too deeply.

And I often shit my pants, proverbially speaking, in pursuit of excellent outcomes. In the process, I learn lessons, whether they be about R&D teams or about morning commutes.

You've never heard of me. And there's a good reason for that! I'm not a luminary. I'm not a titan of industry. I'm not a wunderkind. I have no quotes on leadership that appeal to courage; my inspirational quote would be more like:

A leader shits their pants trying to get through Atlanta traffic to work.

Not sure that's terribly inspiring.

I'm just a guy who's had to lead for a long time. And I've failed *a lot*, gastrointestinally and otherwise. And I've succeeded sometimes! Reviewing my progress throughout the years, I've gotten better at leading over time. I've learned some things that have allowed me to get better at making decisions for teams and companies.

What I've learned is generalizable. As in, anyone who wants to be a better leader can engage in these things I've learned over the years. More to the point, they can engage with the stuff in this book *without having to be someone else*. There will be very little in this book about changing your voice Elizabeth Holmes–style, drinking your coffee with MCT oil in it, low-dosing psychedelics, or whatever the new on-surface leadership performance tactic might be. My goal is that you can learn a thing or two about leadership from this book and apply it at your job *while still being yourself*—maybe even a better version of yourself, rather than trying to get you to be someone else entirely. One of my employees once called me an "equal opportunity asshole," so I'm definitely not going to try to get you to behave like me.

So why do I think I'm capable of writing a leadership book especially given that just a year ago, I was scared to talk to my own managers about the topic? Here are my basic qualifications:

- **I'm an OK writer:** Most leadership books are nauseatingly dull. I don't even know how people got through them before the 1.5x audiobook speed button was invented back in the early naughts. They're almost impossible to get through unless Alvin and the Chipmunks are your narrators. I swear to you this book will be 20 percent more interesting than any other leadership book you've bought in the airport bookstore. Why am I confident of this? My previous book was about Microsoft Excel (Not sorry. Excel is the best!), but the preponderance of the reviews say it's 20 percent more interesting than other stuff about Excel, and if I can make spreadsheets interesting, I can make business leadership interesting. Hell, more often than not, leadership and spreadsheets may be the same things in modern times.

- **I know some fiddly academic things:** I have a background in decision-making. I have a graduate degree in it from MIT (math applied to decision-making, specifically). And I worked as a consultant helping some of the largest organizations in the world make decisions using math. I wrote a book about decision-making (from a mathy perspective) called *Data Smart*. So when I talk about decision-making in leadership, I'm not *purely* shooting from the hip. Only kinda from the hip? I'm shooting from the midriff, let's say. The midriff is in style again fashion-wise, right? Ka-chow!

- **I've seen some shit:** I was the chief product officer for Mailchimp and helped build a product that eventually commanded a $12 billion purchase price from Intuit. And currently, I'm the chief product officer at Podium. We're currently valued at about $3 billion. That's a lot of value to be responsible for! As a tech executive, "life comes at you fast." Every week there are tons of decisions to make. Hiring and firing, forming teams and dissolving teams, building products and sunsetting them, moving money around, deciding which customers to make happy and which to piss off. I've seen a lot, and I've had to make thousands and thousands of decisions, some of them quite important.

- **I've failed:** Too many business books are written solely from a place of strength to prop up the ego of the author. That's cool. But that's not this. I've made so many bad decisions I've lost count. If you don't believe me, please know that *I have a neck tattoo.* That's how committed to bad decisions I seem to be. Gotta practice what you preach! Failure is how we learn.

- **I've succeeded too:** But I don't want to fetishize failure! We fail so that *we can do better.* Those who fail for failure's sake and cite bullshit like "90 percent of Google's experiments fail!" are so tiresome. They'd A/B their own wedding night if they could. They've become so enamored with failure that they no longer seek to win. I fail, but I've failed while trying to win. I shit my pants, but at least I'm trying to make the meeting when I do! And I've kept my eyes open when I fail, taken note of why, and done better next time. My hope is to pass on those learnings to you.

Those are my basic qualifications, such as they are. Let's get to it.

What's a Leader?

A leader is a dealer in hope.

—Napoleon Bonaparte

A leader is one who knows the way, goes the way, and
shows the way.

>   —John Maxwell

The first responsibility of a leader is to define reality. The last
is to say thank you. In between, the leader is a servant.

>   —Max DePree

The function of leadership is to produce more leaders, not
more followers.

>   —Ralph Nader

A true leader has the confidence to stand alone, the courage to
make tough decisions, and the compassion to listen to the
needs of others.

>   —Douglas MacArthur

There are thousands of quotes on what a leader is. Often,
these quotes are from famous leaders waxing poetically on leadership (their own job!), which in a way feels quite convenient; it's
a circular kind of compliment. Like if I as a product manager
said, "Product leadership is being awesome every day," that would
be convenient given I'm a product manager. I must be awesome
every day!

Taking merely the previous quotes, we can surmise that a
leader is a hope-dealing, human GPS wayfinding, reality defining (whoa), leader producing, courageous loner. If I were to create a Venn diagram of all the leadership quotes out there and try
to paint a picture of that which lies at their intersection, I think
I'd be left with some cross between Morpheus from *The Matrix*
and Queen Elizabeth II.

Imagine defining the words "tennis player" as "Serena
Williams." Pretty unhelpful as a definition! But that's what so
many folks who pontificate on leadership are doing basically.
They're painting an idealized, often personality-driven picture

of *world-class leadership* assuming we already know what basic leadership is and have the simple mechanics down. Funny thing is (and this is the secret you and I will share in this book), a great leader is often an average person, like you or me, who just got really stinking good at the basic mechanics of leadership—mechanics that anyone can master.

By the way, Williams says, "The most important thing in a leader is ownership." As far as quotes go, this isn't a bad one, although I would disagree. The most important thing is, on balance, making good decisions over time. Ownership ranks high but not number one.

I'm so tired of folks telling me how a leader is supposed to *come off.* Aren't you? They're probably not wrong all the time. But they are *unhelpful.* As we'll get into later in this book, telling someone to be courageous directly or confident directly or charismatic directly is, at worst impossible if that's not their personality. And at best, the way to instill those qualities in the person is best done not by leadership training suppository (I tell you to be charismatic at a conference or an off-site and then you just cosplay being courageous and maybe it sticks) but through a more circuitous process of behavior modification that we'll touch on in a later chapter.

So. . .what is a leader? Let's define it!

A leader is someone who makes decisions for a group of people to accomplish a goal.

That's the definition I'm gonna use in this book. Is it the best definition? Probably not. But! At least this is a definition that just about anyone *regardless of personality, identity, background, or affinity for black turtlenecks* can get behind.

Based on this definition, then like I said earlier in response to Williams:

A great leader is someone who makes repeated good decisions over time.

Let me ask you a question: who's a better leader? Someone who has charisma, taste, unassailable character, and sharp wit, and is exceptionally decisive *but* they tend to make bad decisions? Or someone who's a bit less charismatic, not awesome in front of the whole company, has a degree of "moral flexibility," and a bad haircut *but* they make consistently good decisions? Case in point: Jimmy Carter. President Carter is without a doubt one of the finest Americans to ever walk this planet; just look at his work with Habitat for Humanity. Was he a great leader? Most historians would say no. He has an unassailable character but a moderate track record on making good calls.

The purpose of this book is not to create a funhouse version of yourself that looks more like General Patton by the time we're done. I'm going to assume if you're reading past this point, as this is a "business leadership book" (ew), that you're in business and have to make decisions for a group of people to accomplish goals. And the purpose of this book is to make you a better decision-maker.

That's what businesses need. Courage is awesome. Grit is awesome. Vision-casting is awesome! But we all have different strengths as leaders. What unites us at a base level is that *we all have to make decisions that affect other people.* Why not just get better at that? I contend that if you can get really good at just that, your performance as a leader will jump at least one whole letter grade.

So many leaders work on their behaviors, personality, and image, while ignoring the fact that they're shit decision-makers. They're just slinging bad decisions all day long. Over time they become better speakers, more efficient users of their time, better rested, more mindful, whatever, while remaining shit decision-makers. All good things, but becoming a more charismatic shit decision-maker is actually a negative for the company! The last thing we need is someone who's better at leading people off of cliffs. Nothing is more dangerous than someone who plays the idealized aspects of a leader well but chooses the wrong answer time and time again. Additionally, these leaders often think they're right because they're "playing the part" of the leader so well. They're dressed like rock stars, but they can't play an instrument to save their life.

Case in point: Al Dunlap, otherwise known as "Chainsaw Al."

Why was Dunlap called "The Chainsaw?" Was he a pro wrestler? Nope, although I'm sure he fancied himself as one. Dunlap was known for using mass layoffs to make a company's books attractive again. And he embraced that single tactic as some kind of all-encompassing philosophy, once posing with an ammo belt across his chest. Rather than learn how to be a good leader (which, in my opinion, is to *make demonstrably good decisions repeatedly over time*), Dunlap just kept on hitting that "fire" button. It worked for a time until he took over as CEO of Sunbeam in 1996. He laid off a bunch of folks, made Sunbeam extremely profitable in the short term, but when he couldn't find a buyer for the leaner company, he was forced to run Sunbeam for the long haul. Those who storm beaches aren't necessarily good at occupying, especially when their only tool is an unwieldy chainsaw and ammo belt (why not pose with a chainsaw? Chainsaws don't use ammo! I'm so confused). Dunlap couldn't figure out what to do when he wasn't firing people.

To make a long story short, Dunlap ended up having to commit fraud to make Sunbeam look good when his chainsaw didn't work.

Let's not be like Dunlap.

This book isn't going to be about chainsaws and ammo belts (although occasionally a chainsaw may be required. Layoffs are a decision that we sometimes have to make). This is a book about

A FEW THINGS UP FRONT

making good decisions repeatedly over time. That's it. If it sounds kind of bland, sorry, not sorry! It's bland like butter; you don't eat straight butter (unless you're a Lab...more on that later), but it makes everything else better.

In my experience, those who try to artificially inflate leadership to be some kind of spiritual, emotional, and moral battlefield on a daily basis are the same people who refuse to get into the weeds when they need to, refuse to learn basic subject matter, and make calls on things like how to performance manage, allocate staff, spend a budget, etc. They refuse to look at data, and they refuse to learn lessons. Those who are overly focused on leadership as a practice that never touches the mundane are often the worst, cockiest, and most impractical leaders one can find.

So onward! Let's get exceedingly dull in this book! Make yourself a cup of tea, put on some reading glasses, and put away your ammo belt.

1

Business Books Suck

We've all been there. Your manager or the CEO or the head of HR has read a new business book. God help us.

All of a sudden, there they are on stage in the company all-hands meeting, gesticulating like a madperson, talking about some dude who climbed Everest and dropping bombs about what it's like to make decisions when you're "low on oxygen in white-out conditions."

Hold up. . .Everest is now floating in the ocean? Ohhh! It's now a floating glacier. We've gone maritime. We're talking about how 80 percent of glaciers are below the surface—"people, processes, and technology." You're trying to keep up with the shifting metaphor, but you're drowning in the cold, glacial sea of this all-hands rant.

Now we're on a boat sailing toward the glacier? Or maybe it's the competition sailing at us and we're the glacier? Someone is about to hit this glacier; it's unclear who at this point.

When the town hall is over, the leader has basically given the world's worst business book report disguised as a motivational speech. Meanwhile, you've gotta trot back to your desk and make heads or tails of how ramping a glacier in a Zodiac boat is supposed to change how you allocate your budget across hiring and software spend. Good luck.

Do business books ever make our lives better? Or do they just lead to the world's worst company all-hands meetings and even worse decision-making? We've all been "managed by a business book," which is worse than having to read the book yourself.

But why do business books suck so bad? Oh, let me count the ways.

1. **"Swoop and poop" by analogy books:** These books often derive their authority from things that have nothing to do with your day-to-day leadership experience. The author is a mountain climber turned entrepreneur, they're a professional athlete turned venture capitalist, they're a military hero turned motivational speaker who sleeps four hours a night but it's OK because they're pinning a gram of exogenous testosterone on the regular.

   Ninety percent of their leadership advice comes from their former life, which they try to translate from the football pitch to the boardroom. It doesn't work, much the same way my experience caring for a corgi doesn't make me qualified to write a parenting book. You probably know more than these people about leading in your actual job. They're just "swooping and pooping" little nuggets of wisdom from another field like "When visibility on the mountain is low, trust your team/ training/coach/instincts" and hoping it lands. It's like a horoscope—vague enough that they rely on you to make the connections to your job. But they'll take credit if it all works out for you. If the advice doesn't work out, well, you misapplied it.

2. **"Great businessman" books:** I use the word *man* here because it so often is some dude. These books at least are written by someone in business. Often for them lightning has struck once, maybe twice. Maybe more. And they're telling their story of success mixed with a bit of learnings and takeaways. They simplify a complex tale that led to their success in order to produce a myth of themselves that comes complete with takeaways for you to try. The cast of characters is reduced. Errors are minimized. Right decisions are distilled to general principles.

   Too often, the takeaways are overly specific to *someone with their personality*. Oh, you worked 100-hour weeks and slept in the office? You likely were already a Disc D, Enneagram 3 or 8, ENTJ hard-charger. You took some time off when faced with your next challenge and went to Burning Man? Cool bro. Sometimes these books veer off into historical figure worship as do so many business books: throw in a little "Churchill slept only 4 hours a night" or "Jobs wore the same thing every day to streamline his life."

   These books leave the reader wrestling with whether their success as a leader is predicated on a seemingly impossible personality and behavioral transformation.

   You know that guy Al Dunlap I talked about in the introduction who executed a large accounting fraud when his "chainsaw" tactics failed him? Before the SEC investigated him, he published a *New York Times* bestseller titled *Mean Business: How I Save Bad Companies and Make Good Companies Great*. You see the "I" in that title? That's that "great businessman" type of book I'm talking about.

3. The **academic study "insight porn" as unifying theory of leadership book:** These suckers are at least grounded in more than just a singular experience. But they'll often take a single study or a single survey and blow it out of proportion.

These books use "insight porn" tactics where the study being cited gives a nonintuitive result that shocks the reader into reevaluating all that they know. There's a mountaintop guru a-ha moment. Do more by doing less, lead from behind, the best defense is a good offense, etc. They turn the world on its head. It can be a fun format!

Hey, it's really interesting that on sales teams if you promote a high performer to manager, you're just as likely to fail as if you promote a low performer or hire from the outside. But can we really apply that to all hiring and promotion in all disciplines? Perhaps product management or technology management have nothing to do with sales management. Since I'm in a vague, nonquota trade, I'm pretty sure the takeaways aren't generalizable.

These kinds of books can be educational and helpful but also dangerous because they hand you an academically backed chainsaw, a singular tool or worldview that you can now apply to all situations and appear enlightened. But remember, academic studies often use analogs to generalize findings. There are studies that use how well mice swim as an analog for the efficacy of antidepressants in humans. Let's be reasonable in how much we allow academic studies to generalize what it means to be good leaders in business. (I say this as someone who really likes academia and enjoys a good study.)

4. **Super Soul Sunday turned business book:** These are similar to the academic books mentioned. You take someone on the periphery of business leadership, perhaps an executive coach or psychologist, and have them create a "unifying theory of leadership" that centers around behavior, personal growth, and psychological phenomena. The formula is something like this: take a trendy self-help/self-care topic, like

how to process shame, how to have better conversations in the midst of conflict, or techniques for handling anxiety, and project those insights onto the entirety of business as the key to unlock successful and sustainable outcomes.

The insights can often be helpful but only tangentially. It's like nutrition. The primary drivers of health are big things like total calorie intake, macronutrient distribution, sleep, and exercise. Micronutrients like vitamin C matter secondarily (no one wants scurvy!), but you better believe there's a book out there on how vitamin C is the secret to everything. The business world is full of such things: micro-insights around personality and behavior being projected into macro-insights. Meditation is an excellent tool for leaders, but I know tons of excellent leaders who do not meditate. So let's not make that the key to becoming better.

The truth is that each and every one of these books has a few nuggets that are likely helpful! I've read plenty of business books in each of these categories and have benefitted to a degree.

How many of you have ever read a business book and found it helpful in most hard business situations going forward? So helpful that you're able to remember that thing you listened to at 1.5x speed even a year later? The shelf life of a business book inside that skull of yours is probably "until I read the next business book."

These things have limited applicability, because their grand theories are based on specific truths too small to encompass all that leadership entails in our context. Furthermore, acting as though their limited and narrow takeaways are universal keys to business success actually leads these books to be less helpful! Their word count increases, and they strain the bounds of how their takeaways might be metaphorically (mis)applied. And all of a sudden, a 3,000-word essay on time management becomes a 50,000-word grand theory on organizational efficiency as the secret sauce to success.

Business books suck not in that their small nuggets are wrong but in that they try to make their small nuggets everything!

So if that's the case, what's the alternative?

Context Is Everything: Do Things That [Don't?] Scale

I was raised in the conservative evangelical church during the 90s. And at that time there was a phrase that struck fear into the hearts of all evangelicals: "moral relativism." This is the idea that what is right and what is wrong is "relative" to the context you're in. If picking your nose is wrong, the 90s evangelical church would say it's *always* wrong! The heroes of the church were the uncompromising—William Wallace came up *a lot*. Not the historical figure, mind you, mostly just Mel Gibson's uncompromising portrayal. Either you could be a "person of principle" or you could be Machiavelli.

It's easy to see why such an approach to religious education is attractive. What's going to produce more "reliable" results? Encouraging folks to engage critically and contextually with the world or giving folks a set of rules by which they must act in every situation without question? For a lot of folks, there's relief in the clarity provided by rigidity. Personal responsibility is lifted when you're made into a dogmatic robot.

It's not just the 90s evangelical church that doesn't like relativism, or, as this book will put it, **contextual decision-making**. Westerners generally, religious or not, *really do not like relativism* as a rule. Why? We like everything to be organized and logical;

we like the advice we're given to be boiled down to a set of "if, then" statements. If this happens, then do this. Works every time.

This reduces doubt and personal responsibility. It doesn't matter whether we're talking cooking, religion, child rearing, or business. We all love a good instruction manual.

I have some good friends who recently had a child, and they signed up for a service called "Moms on Call," which they paid for well into their kid's toddler years. The service had a fascinating business model: call us, and we'll tell you what to do.

Parenting is scary! It's some of the hardest leadership many of us will ever engage with. Lots of ambiguity. Lots of complexity. Stakes are very high; another person is depending on you for everything! People just want to know *what do I do*. And so Moms on Call provides direct answers, it provides instructions, increases confidence, and reduces responsibility. Phew!

And at the heart of all these business books, we find the same phenomenon: **a market rising up to meet the demand for instruction manuals in the face of uncertainty**. Business books try to give you specific rules to live by 100 percent of the time. Go harder, lean in, amp it up. Engage in conflict like this. Manage employees like that.

In a way, business books *have to be this way*. After all, who wants to buy a book whose advice is, "it depends?"

Well, suckers, got you! I hope you checked this out from the library because if you paid for this thing and were expecting a list of instructions, you just wasted a couple bucks! You see, the whole premise of this book is: *it depends*. Context is king.

But let me show you that you already believe this. Deep down, you know that there's no rigid framework, however complex, that can be applied to make a good decision in every context.

Paul Graham, tech billionaire and Y Combinator founder, once said, "Do things that don't scale." Everyone loves that quote in the tech startup world. It means that you should be inefficient and ramp up fast to figure out whether something is going to work, have product market fit, etc. Often this is translated into "throwing bodies" at a problem that should be scaled technologically, but you just don't want to spend the time on that until you know whether it's worth it.

Makes sense, right? I do this all the time! Recently, at Podium, where, as CPO, I'm responsible for our product road map, we launched a VoIP system for local businesses. Our phone system is awesome because it integrates with all the other software we offer, such as texting, payments, marketing, etc. When the customer calls in, we pop open a caller ID that gives the business all the information they need about the caller (what have they purchased, did they review you on Google, what did you last chat about, etc.). What business wouldn't want that? But changing out a phone system, well, that's a pain in the ass.

Changing phone systems has all sorts of operational complexities for local businesses, so we threw Podium bodies at the problem. All sorts of folks with different job titles jumped in to help early customers test their network speeds, port their phone lines to Podium, and change over their phone hardware to our new service. We knew that wouldn't scale efficiently. But we did it anyway to learn fast. Before you spend millions of dollars and person hours writing code, maybe you should see whether the new go-to-market motion you're trying even works!

Counterpoint: "Do things *that scale*," says Parker Conrad, founder of Zenefits and Rippling. I'm pretty sure he's a billionaire too. We have a battle of billionaire adages, folks!

Parker tried doing "things that don't scale" at Zenefits. He found that then going back and scaling operations efficiently that had already been ossified using human labor was often intractable. In the effort to scale fast, humans create systems that are difficult to replace with machines later (after all, we like job security!). So at his next company, he decided the best way to go was to do things right from the get-go. He built Rippling on code, not warm bodies.

Do things that scale. That pays off in the long term. Makes sense.

So! Which is right?

Honestly, they're **both true even though they contradict each other**. There are contexts where you should throw bodies at a problem to test something, and there are contexts where that creates more problems than it solves.

But what business book is going to say, "Y'all, do things that don't scale unless that's gonna get you in trouble later, and in that case, do things that scale."?

Well, this book is going to say that later, so let me rephrase that question: what business book that wants to sell more than 10 copies to the author's family members would ever say such a thing? (Hi, Mom!)

It's not that business books are wrong or right. It's that they're often right *some of the time*. But they purport to be right *all of the time*. And so you can't become a better leader by reading one. You've got to read a business book, read its opposite, and then be the kind of leader who knows when to pull from which book!

This subtle shift from "right some of the time" to "right in all contexts" is at the core of why business books suck. Business books create leaders who are a dangerous combination of the following:

- **Inattentive:** Takes the responsibility off the leader to fully understand a situation and be judicious in that moment. They simply pattern match to the business book they like and then shoot from the hip.

- **Overconfident:** "Right in some contexts" provides options
  for a leader. It makes them more equipped. "Right in all contexts" simply makes a leader overconfident that they have
  the answers.

Inattentive yet overconfident leaders are truly the worst.
I bet if you look around in your personal life and in the broader
business world and in politics and in religion and on and on,
you'll see that it's these inattentive yet overconfident blowhards
that we so often laud.

Additionally, there's another confounding issue with business
books: confirmation bias. Guess who tends to buy business books
that claim success lies merely in leaning in and working harder?
People who already drive hard!

Guess who tends to buy business books that claim success
lies in the softer side of things, like empathetic leadership and
having difficult but necessary conversations? Folks already prone
to self-reflection and leadership by relationship!

The people who bought Al "The Chainsaw" Dunlap's *Mean
Business* were the folks who like wielding chainsaws. We buy
management books that affirm our tendencies rather than books
that challenge us.

This leads to a leader whose bag of tools for solving problems specializes and calcifies over time rather than creating leaders who pull from tools they didn't even know about a couple
years prior.

Business books have created echo chambers where specialist
leaders hear what they want to hear and keep acting the way
they've always acted. It's a recipe for a glacier metaphor in a town
hall, and nobody wants that.

What If I Said That Bad Leaders Are Too Consistent?

The leadership personas we laud in business are all mythical. Jobs, Carnegie, Walton, you name them, none of them real.

The images we've created of them in order to make snackable leadership models out of them are images that are far too *monolithic*. They become archetypes who often behave in our literature the same way in each situation.

Jobs wore the same thing every day, ate the same thing, was always difficult to please, was always design-first (business and functionality be damned), etc.

Chris Rock has a famous stand-up routine where he talks about how every time he had an ailment or an injury, his dad would just recommend Robitussin. Cancer? Robitussin. Broken leg? Rub some Robitussin on it.

It's an absurd and hilarious portrait of a father taking a thing with limited applications and making it a panacea. But that's literally *what bad leaders do*.

Because what's another way to describe a leader who behaves the same way in all circumstances?

That's a leader who doesn't hear people. That's a leader who doesn't learn. That's a leader who's unwilling to "get into the weeds."

It's a garbage leader.

Yet those caricatures are our heroes. What should we take away from the nearly fictionalized Churchill who *never gave up?* Well, considering your job isn't fighting nazis but might be building enterprise SaaS software, I'd hope not much.

When I was a boy, I liked to play *Street Fighter 2* with my older brother. *Street Fighter* is a two-player fighting game similar to *Mortal Kombat*. I sucked so bad at *Street Fighter 2*. So every time we played, I'd just take my character, crouch down, and try to "sweep the leg" of my brother à la *Karate Kid*. Let's just say that my competition got wise to me. My older brother learned to just jump the sweep and kick me in the head. I lost over and over and over again. Consistency led me not to victory but to defeat.

The authoritarian leader in all contexts is an asshole.

The servant leader in all contexts has abdicated their authority.

The "in-the-weeds" leader in all contexts is a micromanager and a control freak.

The "30,000-foot" leader in all contexts is out of touch and probably kinda stupid.

The people-first leader in all contexts is likely to drive cancerously high employee retention and free riding.

The performance-first leader in all contexts is likely to drive burnout and high turnover.

OK, you're probably tracking at this point.

Business books are echo chambers that create unhealthy levels of leadership "consistency" leading to bad outcomes for all involved.

Introducing Wisdom Literature

"Do things that don't scale." Absolutely.

"Do things that scale." Yup. On board.

What's going on?

Well, I propose that there's a whole genre of literature that's more helpful than business books for understanding how, so often, a piece of advice and its opposite can be helpful. And that genre is called *wisdom literature*. I first learned about wisdom literature from talking with my wife who's a pastor and who reads

Hebrew and Greek and stuff. She talked me through this whole genre of literature, and it was extremely foreign to me, a boring old businessperson. As a pastor, she was faced with considering moral dilemmas (the hardest of decision-making problems) all the time, but the literature she was pulling from was absolutely not written by Al "The Chainsaw" Dunlap. She kept referring to the ancient wisdom texts instead.

Wisdom literature originated thousands of years ago in the ancient near east (ANE). And its purpose was to turn little princes into future wise rulers. But it didn't necessarily do this through telling these little princes what to do. Instead, it had them struggle with tough dilemmas. You don't build bigger muscles by watching an instructional video; you build bigger muscles by getting under the bar and struggling yourself!

Take, for example, the "Dialogue between a Man and His God," which is a text written in Akkadian on a clay tablet from 1600s BCE Babylon. The author of the text wrestles with why a god that he worships and sacrifices to permits evil to happen to him. It's an age-old question: why do bad things happen to good people? Young princes needed to wrestle with the seeming injustice inherent in life itself.

And guess what? *The answer is never given* as to why this god has permitted their servant to suffer! The tablet merely lays out that this kind of thing happens. It's up to the reader then to wrestle with the implications.

Wisdom literature as a genre is more interested in giving the reader a headache, destabilizing their confidence and their surety, than it is in giving them pat answers to problems. Wisdom literature creates humility in the face of the unsolvable. It created young princes who recognized that there were going to be problems in life (like the anger of the gods) for which no amount of Robitussin would suffice.

And that humility makes for good leadership.

Source: Historien spécialiste du bassin minier du Nord-Pas-de-Calais JÄNNICK Jérémy / Wikimedia Commons / Public Domain. (GNU Free Documentation License)

The Facebook Uncle Dilemma

Why gods permit suffering isn't terribly handy as a topic for this book. That's a different section of Barnes & Noble. Instead, let's turn our attention to your crazy uncle. I know you've got one. We all do these days.

Uncle Carl is on Facebook. Oh no. He's talking about how "the politicians are in league with the lizard people to hide the fact that the world is actually flat." He's linking to dubious sites. I'm pretty sure all of them are trying to install malware while also peddling conspiracies.

His most recent post has really gotten under your skin. He's suggesting a local leader, maybe your church's pastor, your mayor, your dean, is in league with this reptilian, otherworldly enemy that somehow has something to do with George Soros. You feel yourself getting a little hot under the collar.

What do you do in response to your uncle?

In business book land, you could find a book that would say something like this:

"Don't suffer fools gladly!"

Nothing like some King James Corinthians for figuring out your approach to Facebook uncles. I put that quote in Comic Sans to prevent you from photographing it and posting it to your Instagram story as inspiration for the masses.

Meanwhile, back in business book land, you could easily find another book that would say this:

Never wrestle with a pig. You both get dirty, and the pig likes it.

Cool. Don't wrestle pigs, but don't suffer fools.

Well, wisdom literature as a genre would simply nod its head at both viewpoints. Let's look at the book of *Proverbs*, one of the most famous wisdom literature books of all time, which is part of the *Ketuvim* in the Hebrew Bible.

Proverbs 26:4-5:

Answer not a fool according to their folly, lest you be like them yourself.

Answer a fool according to their folly, lest they be wise in their own eyes.

So. . .don't answer your uncle. Don't be brought down to his level! After all, it'll just validate him that somehow his position is credible enough to deign arguing with.

Wait. . ."answer a fool?" I thought Proverbs just said not to answer him! OK, so you've got to answer him so that he doesn't go on making an ass of himself. Or hell, your grandma reads his posts. . .maybe you need to answer him just so she sees that not everyone agrees with his hot takes.

The purpose of wisdom literature isn't to tell you *what to think*. It's to give you **options**, experiences, and spectrums of action. The rest is up to you! Wisdom literature, unlike business books, admits that life is complex, and the situations you find yourself in require a nuanced understanding of the context in order to act.

Only you know how your uncle might react. Only you know who else is reading his posts and commenting on them who might be deceived. Only you know if you have a good enough relationship with your uncle that he might be receptive to your words.

So as a leader, you get to decide which *option* to apply in this circumstance.

That's what it means to be a leader. That's why a robot that's read a bunch of business books will forever suck at leading. You have to understand what's going on in the moment just as well as you need to understand that audiobook you listened to on your commute if you're going to make the right call.

Modern business books often give knowledge, which is to say specific pieces of information (facts, processes, frameworks) useful for **deterministic** decision-making.

Wisdom literature, I'd contend, acknowledges that in a complex world, leaders don't make deterministic decisions. We play with *probabilities* in complex situations with imperfect information. We do this by collecting and evaluating *options*. You're going to hear the word *option* a lot in this book.

Recently, I had two "B-players" on my team at work. Now, we've all heard the phrase "A-players only" in business. Netflix is perhaps most famous for its "A-players only" hiring and firing practices. There's probably a book or two out there touting the principle. I like it! But nevertheless, I had hired two Bs. What was I going to do with them?

Should I just take the principle and apply it writ large? One of the B players seemed to be stuck in amber. No matter how much coaching they received, they remained a B. Good, not great.

The other B player was trending down, but when given feedback, they got their ass in gear and were moving up into B+ territory. With the former, we fired them. With the latter, we merely told them they weren't cutting it, but we envisioned that they could make it to an A if they applied themselves. They acknowledged they'd been a little checked out, and their heart wasn't in it. In the end, they chose to leave the business of their own accord.

You see, a business book will tell you to fire a D player. They'll even tell you to generally fire the B player. But what about that *specific* B player you have? The one who used to be an A and then their job description changed based on company needs. Are they trending back up? Trending down? Holding steady? Maybe their failure to adapt is your fault? They just need training. They just need a plan, etc., etc. We've entered the realm of complex decision-making. This is where we leave our books somewhat behind, and we're on our own.

This isn't to say that wisdom literature is the only place we see such an outlook on the world. Maybe wisdom persists today. . .just not in business books. After all, Kenny Rogers didn't say "hold 'em!" Instead, he presented the options.

You've gotta know when to hold 'em, know when to fold 'em.

Those are the options. And it's on you based on the context to decide. Ack! Poker relativism! Bad Kenny. Bad.

In my opinion, the best leaders, the "wise" leaders, are ones who engage well in **options-based decision-making**, which is to say, nondeterministic decision-making processes. Robotic leaders often fail, especially in situations in which the context rapidly shifts such that the game being played is different from month to month and year to year.

Good leadership is dynamic and contextual. Done well, that's what it means to have "wisdom!" It's beyond knowledge, beyond frameworks, beyond doing the same thing every time because that's how you've been trained.

And that sets up our next chapter. Let's illustrate with examples why there really is *no shake-and-bake way to lead.*

CHAPTER

2

Let's Warm Up! Ten Business Choices Where One Option and Its Opposite Both Have Merit

Years ago I joined CrossFit like every other 30-year-old geriatric millennial out there who wanted to get in shape. And for a while, I thought I was doing well! I would do a workout at the gym and not die. I'd be miserable, but eventually I got to where I could breathe after the workout was done. Sometimes, I'd even muster the fitness level required to best my wife in a workout, although that was rare if I'm being honest.

We all know how this short CrossFit story ends, right? It ended where all CrossFit stories end: with a back injury.

One day, I pulled a 400-pound deadlift, and I felt something in my back *give a little*. As humans, we generally just think of our body as, well, a singular thing, which is to say an integrated thing that just all fits together. So when a piece of that body moves somewhere it's not supposed to, it's always a tad disconcerting, like when a tire flies off your car as you barrel down the freeway— that kind of disconcerting.

I dropped the barbell when it happened and just walked away. I'd pulled a muscle really badly in my lower-left side. The pain was so bad that for a couple of weeks it hurt to even sit. I remember being in excruciating pain during my kids' Christmas pageant where I kept wondering whether frankincense or myrrh had analgesic properties. I would've robbed baby Jesus of his gifts if it'd have helped with the pain. I was in a bad way.

As it turns out, I (like many CrossFitters) had reached a point where my strength had outstripped my intelligence and, in particular, my training and form. I was lifting too much with my lower back and not enough from my hamstrings, and I ended up looking like my dog when he takes a dump (that question mark shape dogs make) every time I lifted.

After that injury, did I learn? Nope. I let it heal and then went back to what I was doing. I pulled the same muscle again. And again. And again. As I said in the foreword of this book, I'm no genius.

I kept pulling that muscle until I *finally* received coaching on how to move my body (or in the case of my core, which should have been stiffer, *not move my body*) while lifting. The coach broke down my lift into little pieces and showed me how to do the movement better and safer. I had to build my muscle memory back up from scratch to perform the movement *right*. I wasn't as strong in this new position at first, but in the end, I grew stronger and successfully avoided injury.

When it comes to making decisions as leaders, *we all have muscle memory*. We've built it up over the years. We favor using the muscles that seem strongest to us (lifting with our back as it were), i.e., strengths that we've accumulated over the years via natural disposition of our personality, training, and experience. Experience in particular acts as a feedback loop (something we'll discuss later in this book) causing our decision-making to ossify because as humans we are pattern matchers and hardwired to avoid previous *pain* (failure).

A few years back my family was vacationing in Turks and Caicos, which has to be as close to heaven as this earth gets, and my niece jumped off a rock that was about 40 feet above the ocean. She hit the water wrong and got herself a bruise that ran from her butt to the back of her knee. Ouch!

Years later, every time she gets close to the edge of a ledge like that, she gets butterflies and a little tingly. It's her brain matching a pattern and her body telling her to avoid previous pitfalls. Hell, that's the same reason I can't drink coconut LaCroix anymore. My brain thinks if I do, I'll shit my pants! Danger!

Pattern matching is a good thing. Aeschylus put it like this, "Memory is the mother of all wisdom." I disagree, but I get his point. Over time as leaders we accumulate training and experiences that allow us to see situations for what they are, avoid pitfalls, and make decisions quickly to guide a team in the right direction. It works! Right up until it doesn't. Right up until the world changes, our pattern matching doesn't work great, and we pull a proverbial back muscle.

For example, my pattern matching brain tells me to scream and run away whenever a software engineer says "replatform" or "rearchitect" or "refactor." The three "Re's" of the software apocalypse always meant wasted time in my experience. And yet, this past year members of the Podium R&D team more or less gave me a "come to Jesus" talk about the need to "rearchitect our mobile app." My muscle memory told me not to listen to the options they laid out. But the world had changed for mobile, and our app just wasn't cutting it. My pattern matching would have had us stay on the old architecture, but what the world (and our customers) demanded from mobile apps had changed; my muscles' preference was untenable.

The team was persuasive, and we reached an agreement. I'd let them proceed with this option for a time, but they had to hit well-articulated checkpoints every few weeks toward a release of a new app. No wandering in the reachitecture wilderness for 40 years!

Boy, am I glad the team argued with me, because they were right. They completed the new app on time and to great reviews in the App Store. Our customers were happy. My fears were proven wrong.

This chapter is all about *breaking down our muscle memory*.

Each of us has a go-to solution to various business problems, but as I said in the previous chapter, so often there's an opposite and equally valid solution to that same problem.

I'm not saying that your go-to solution *is always wrong*. It's not! Hell, it may be right most of the time. But what I am saying is that by considering and thinking through a spectrum of options for solving an important problem, a spectrum that often contains a reasonable yet contradictory approach to your muscle memory, even if we choose to go with Old Standby, we'll be able to articulate the costs of that decision, and the trades we're making will become explicit rather than implicit (or rather denied altogether). And in that consideration, you may find yourself wisely going against your own grain more often than you think.

Let's Take a "Walk Around the Business"

To that end, we're going to take a walk around the common problem types we face as leaders in business. And for each problem, we'll see that two *opposite* options (there's that word again!) often exist. There'll be an "answer a fool" and an "answer not a fool." And let's get comfortable with that. Uncertainty is uncomfortable, but the best leaders I've met have grown more comfortable with uncertainty and ambiguity over time. This chapter and the rest of this book is going to help you out there.

To organize our walk around the business, I'm going to categorize problems vaguely (honestly, this is hard because everything bleeds together) into People, Process, and Product, which is a high-level categorization of business concerns Marcus Lemonis coined to guide leaders' attention to the things that matter most.

This chapter is by no means exhaustive, but I'm going to take you through apparent tensions and contradictions in major topics inside of each of these three areas. This diagram helps summarize it:

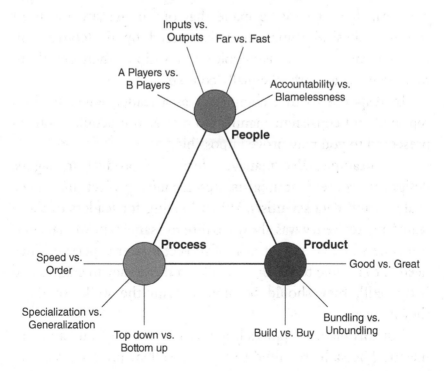

We're going to dive into the 10 topics listed in the diagram, mostly just to show you the variety and trade-offs leaders need to make between opposing "good" ideas in nearly every area of the business. There's no way to cover everything. I'm leaving out all sorts of things about go-to-market, such as pricing and merchandising, but if I were to lay out the contradictions in business decision-making that exhaustively, I'd put you to sleep, and this book would have volumes.

Ten examples will suffice!

People

I can think of no category of business problems that confounds leaders who want to act the same way in each circumstance more than people problems. Why? Because people are the most complex things in the universe. That's not exaggeration. An argument can legitimately be made that our brains are the most complex physical things ever discovered by us (convenient, I know). And that means people's motivations, their emotions, their actions, etc., are all equally complex.

In response to that complexity as a leader, engaging in a repeated and consistent manner no matter the people problem presented to you may prove impossible.

For example, I've managed teams of product managers, designers, content strategists, researchers, project managers, analysts, and data scientists. When looking for leaders of those teams, my tendency was always to hire the same type of manager: someone who had a great deal of subject matter expertise. They needed to be able to "walk the walk" of those they managed, and better still, they should be able to "run the walk" of those they managed.

But this blanket approach ignored all kinds of human complexity. The skills required to be an excellent product manager included managing up and clear communication, so when I hired a director of product management, they tended to handle not just their reports well, but they handled the executive team well. On the flip side, when I took that same approach to hiring a data science director, I didn't get what I'd hoped for. Yes, the director could walk the data science walk. They could clean data and build machine learning models with the best of them, but I hadn't screened primarily for the ability to connect into the business (which isn't the primary skill of a data scientist). Communication outside the team suffered, pursuits became academic, and ultimately, business value was not delivered.

So instead, I brought in a leader for the data science team that was more businessperson, less mathematician. Sometimes they couldn't fully understand the black magic of their data science team. But they could understand the inputs and the outputs. They could manage their people toward the goals of the business. That worked a lot better!

In other words, for me, a director of product management looked a lot like those below them, while a director of data science looked a lot like those above them. I couldn't apply a one-size-fits-all method to my hiring.

People problems! Let's look at a few common ones.

A Players vs. B Players

"A players attract A players. B players attract C players."
—Steve Jobs

Steve Jobs wasn't wrong about that one. Strong performers do attract strong performers. And conversely, in my experience, tolerating average performers does indeed lead to a degradation in overall performance over time.

I once worked at a company that for whatever reason tolerated B players at the top over long periods of time. *B player* might be generous. I once worked with an executive who after a year still couldn't articulate how our product worked and what it did. He was a C player at best, although he was probably getting Cs by copying someone else's homework.

What happened to him?

That executive struggled to make an impact. And he couldn't effectively grow and lead the team under him in concert with the other teams he had to work with. In every company survey that ranked leadership, his team ranked him abysmally low. The entire company suffered for years because of that single decision to keep a B player on.

We've all had a similar experience. We've worked with a boss, had a direct report, or had a peer who was middling-to-garbage in their role. It's a drag. And when you're attempting to get something done *as a team*, not having mutual trust (which is impossible to establish with someone who can't do their job) just grinds things to a halt.

And yet, should we aspire to put A players everywhere? I contend no. Although it kind of depends on what *A player* means.

Let's start with a couple of possibly apocryphal stories I've heard over the years.

There once was a chain of mall-based cookie stores. And they decided they wanted to hire A players to be managers of their stores. They'd heard Steve Jobs' quote and figured there wasn't much difference between an Apple and a cookie.

So they went out and recruited blue-chip MBAs to manage their stores. They had to pay more for these folks, but they figured it'd pay off.

What'd these new managers do?

Often, they tried to innovate, specifically by adding more chocolate chips to the cookie recipe. If I asked you to innovate a chocolate chip cookie, I bet adding more chocolate is something you'd try too. Well, this happened in store after store. The MBA, looking to make a visionary impact, would add in more chocolate chips. Contrary to popular belief, however, more chocolate in a cookie doesn't necessarily make it better for the masses. It certainly was less economical for the chain, chocolate being a fairly expensive ingredient compared to, say, flour. And it provided an inconsistent customer experience between chains.

The chain backed away from their MBA strategy.

On the flip side, some decades ago there was a rental car company that found success specifically by *avoiding A players*. They found that their best rental car center managers came from a pool of middling college graduates who were hungry to prove themselves and put a name brand employer on their résumé. Top-performing college grads with the 4.0 GPA just didn't suit the employer and were likely to attrit rather than demonstrate the hunger and loyalty they received from the middling grad. By hiring those with a 3.0 GPA on graduation and placing them in positions of power, they achieved better manager retention and with it better retained institutional knowledge over time. It became a differentiating strength for the company.

In my own experience, I've witnessed similar phenomena. For example, when it came to hiring customer success employees at one of my previous companies, we often saw that more qualified folks were merely using their role as a steppingstone to apply for other roles inside the company. They said all the right things, but secretly they didn't want to perform the duties of a customer service rep. When we hired "less qualified" folks, once they got the hang of the job and hit their ticket quota reliably, they could stay in seat for years. I referred a guy I knew from the local pizza joint to join the customer service team, and he ended up being one of the longest tenured customer service reps of all time at the company, hitting his goals month after month after month.

Meanwhile, I referred someone with a master's degree onto the team who was a genuinely smart, well-spoken, well-written person. They were imminently qualified for a job of speaking and writing to customers! Within weeks they were miserable because they just wanted to use the role as a steppingstone, and secretly, they felt it was beneath their master's degree. And when the next stone to step to didn't present itself immediately, they didn't know how to work hard enough to meet their ticket quota.

In some roles B players just work better!

Of course, that's because the **face-value B players are actually A players for that role.**

So, it's not necessarily that Steve-o was wrong, so much as it is that a leader must define their terms well rather than relying on the business world's definition of "A player." There's that contextual decision-making thing again!

A player in one job might mean "innovator." In another it means "follows orders." In one it means "moves fast." In another it means being "risk averse." The last thing you need in a financial controller is a move-fast innovative risk-taker. But in a product manager, that might work quite well.

So, a leader must define for themselves what "A" means. . .even if (like in the case of the rental car company) "A" means "B." This is starting to come off like a Christopher Nolan plot. "*A means B* starring Leonardo DiCaprio. . ."

To make matters worse, when you redefine A as B or A as anything other than some standard résumé definition of A, it can be very hard to hire properly! Interviewing is just not that accurate at determining the difference between an A and a B. You can check references, you can talk to mutual acquaintances, etc. But it's all a roll of the dice. That means running excellent performance management.

I once interviewed someone who looked like a great fit for a role. Turns out that they'd lied on their résumé, though; halfway through the process they fessed up, right before we were going to start calling references. They explained the lie and the logic behind it. Humorously, the lie kind of made sense. I didn't blame them.

I decided to hire them anyway. I mean. . .I got arrested for shoplifting when I was younger, so if I held every infraction against people, that'd be a weird position to take. But I kept an eye on the person. Turns out they were an A player! They just needed a shot.

On the flip side, I once hired a product leader who had a blue-chip tech résumé. They interviewed well. They knew all the jargon. They provided great examples of how they solved problems. So I hired them. It became rapidly apparent that the decision was a mistake. They had no curiosity or energy. The team had no confidence in them. Their uninspired work didn't align with company strategy. We fired them.

Having a team of A players means firing B players more than it means hiring A players.

So where does all this leave us? I'm going to leave us with a wisdom literature takeaway to hiring. I'll do one of these for all the sections in this chapter in fact.

Wisdom literature takeaway:

Hire A players.

Except when B players do better in the role.

Then B is A. So I guess still hire A players. But like B-ish A players.

Clear as mud. I wish I was joking.

Accountability vs. Blamelessness

"If someone is always to blame, if every time something goes wrong someone has to be punished, people quickly stop taking risks. Without risks, there can't be breakthroughs."

—Peter Diamandis

Recently, there's been a metric ton of talk around creating great company cultures. I can count no less than five recent popular business books on the topic. And there's one word that pops up again and again and again.

Blameless. As the previous quote points out, if you spend time blaming people for failure, they won't take risks, and then you're dead in the water as a company. Running a "blameless" company or team means allowing folks to fail and learn without fear of reprisal. This creates "psychological safety," leading to better conversations, better learning, and ultimately better team performance.

A great application of this approach is in engineering. When an engineering team debriefs on why a system has failed, blame is often unhelpful if your goal is a truthful recounting of the mistakes that were made so that the entire team can learn how not to break the system in the future.

At Podium, we offer local businesses all the tools they need to operate. That includes payment systems. One of the cool payment features we offer is called *text payments* where the local business can simply send a link via SMS to a customer to get paid. During COVID, text payments were exceptionally helpful. And they're way more secure and less prone to failure than taking someone's credit card number over the phone—gross.

Well, shortly after the launch of our text payments feature, a fraudster called into our sales team, impersonated a real gynecologist's office, set up a Podium payments account, and then processed a bunch of text payment transactions from stolen credit cards into their imposter gynecologist Podium account. They then whisked the money out of their Podium account into their bank account and fled before we knew what was up.

We eventually detected the fraud and got law enforcement involved. But Podium was still held liable for covering the losses from the theft.

When this all was happening, our goals were the following:

- Make sure we shut down any active fraud.
- Understand how the fraudster manipulated Podium (humans, processes, and technology) and harden the company against such future activity.

Given those goals, we needed to treat everyone involved in a blameless fashion. The account executive who was fooled into selling the fake gyno? Blameless. The team that operated the credit card payment processing part of the code base? Blameless. The fraudster? Well, we definitely blamed that guy, but screw him.

And because we executed a blameless retrospective and created psychological safety, everyone banded together to learn and close off the holes in our system.

So what's the opposite approach: run a *blameful* culture? Uh, kind of?

> *"On good teams coaches hold players accountable, on great teams players hold players accountable."*
>
> —*Joe Dumars*

Most folks who watch *The Last Dance*, which is a documentary about Michael Jordan and the 1998 Chicago Bulls, have two takeaways:

- Gee, Michael Jordan sure seems like an asshole.
- The Bulls operated with such a high level of accountability that the team was able to get the very best that each player had to offer.

The '98 Chicago Bulls was a pretty *blameful* team. Michael Jordan made sure each player knew if they screwed up. He held himself to an insanely high standard as well. He didn't tolerate poor performers on the team. There was no psychological safety (or even job security). And in the documentary, you see teammate after teammate of Jordan say basically the same thing: he was an asshole, but he got us to where we needed to be. Toxic? Most definitely. But did any of the players on the '98 Bulls say they would've rather been on some other team or led by some other star player? Not that I heard!

I've led product leaders who've wanted their work to be held blameless similar to the way we treated that financial fraud situation. Indeed, I've worked with product leaders who've *fetishized failure*.

"Did you know that only 1 in 10 of Google's tests ever succeed?"

"9 out of 10 tests fail!"

Failure becomes the destination, not a waypoint to success. But if you're fully satisfied with failure, will you ever try hard enough to learn something valuable that leads to success?

These product leaders would even quote *Batman Begins* at me, "Why do we fall, sir? So that we can learn to pick ourselves up." But they had no interest in picking themselves up for any reason other than to fall again.

Over time I noticed the same thing happen again and again with these product leaders who were focused on blamelessly building, iterating, and releasing products that may or may not succeed:

- Their product releases were often duds, lacking product-market fit. Customers didn't care about the work.

- Their product releases came slowly. Teams were allowed to stretch four weeks' worth of work into twelve. (Here goes the executive demanding the team squeeze more juice out of the same fruit!)

Should we be at all surprised? A product leader who holds themselves and their teams blameless with respect to customer and business impact is less likely to operate with any sense of urgency. And they're less likely to care whether the product is liked by the customer. If no fault will be found in you for failure, would you try quite as hard to succeed?

I found that when I ran a team with a higher level of accountability (specifically, I managed out product leaders who operated with low urgency and fetishized failure more than they sought market success), the results showed. More customers were interviewed before features were built. There was more collaboration with go-to-market teams. Releases performed better in-market. Oddly, the product managers who thrived were often happier than on a fully "psychologically safe" team where poor-performing peers were tolerated. And I didn't have to act like Michael Jordan to do it; no shouting required. I just provided clear standards and managed rigorously against them. You don't need to be an asshole when you're able to simply fire folks who don't measure up to clear standards.

Wisdom literature takeaway:

Run a blameless culture so that people will take more risks.

Run a high-accountability culture so that people will make more impact.

Inputs vs. Outputs

Humans are complex, and yet, we use simple compensation models to incent them to do what the business needs. But what do you incentivize?

One school of thought (popularized by Bill Walsh) is that "the score takes care of itself." If you focus on the fundamentals that build to a successful output, rather than focusing on that output directly, paradoxically you'll see successful outputs more often.

Makes sense though, right?

At Podium, right after COVID struck, we had a situation in which hitting our sales targets was a little more challenging than usual. And the sales managers running around shouting "We've gotta hit, bro," didn't seem to help matters because they were just focusing on the output: making sales. That pressure didn't seem to help a team of employees who were struggling to figure out how to hit the numbers.

So instead, we focused the sales team on inputs and let the outputs take care of themselves. We created goals around unique prospecting and customer calls each day. And calls turned into sales opportunities, and those opps into sales, which we called the "Podium math."

When sales folks took their eyes off the scoreboard and fixed them on the activities they did each day, they tended to put more sales on the board!

So what's the contrasting approach? Well, when you create incentive structures that reward on A because "A drives B," then you should be prepared for perverse incentives, i.e., "gaming the system."

Ever been to Popeyes and gone through the drive-thru to get a bucket of fried chicken? Popeyes ultimately cares about repeat purchasing and customer satisfaction, I'd have to imagine. But what do they measure? They measure drive-thru timing as an input. How long does it take to get a car through the window?

Well, what happens in this case? Employees push the drive-thru time down not by handing customers their chicken faster but by telling the customer to go park in the parking lot and someone will walk their food out to them. Is this more efficient? No, you've got to have an employee collect food and walk it from the building and then walk up to car after car asking, "what did you order?" Is it more hygienic touching a bunch of doors to make this happen? Nope.

This slows down service and leaves drive-thru customers pissed off. That drives down customer retention.

It's a clear example where measuring an input to drive an output creates perverse incentives and actually damages the output!

While "you get what you measure," you still "get what you deserve."

In *Game of Thrones*, when Daenerys asks a witch to heal her husband, he is indeed healed by the witch, but he remains catatonic for the rest of his life. Be careful what you wish for, and that applies to KPIs!

At Podium, we comped our sales folks based on signing up users to products. The problem was that some products were contracted SaaS products (so we knew the absolute minimum amount we'd be paid by the customer, and that amount was far above zero), while others were *usage-based products*. On a usage-based product, we were paid as a company only when the customer used the thing! But sales reps didn't care about usage, only about signing folks up. Turns out we were in a "Popeye's drive-thru" situation where the score absolutely *didn't take care of itself*. The sales rep was winning, but Podium and the customer were both losing!

So we changed our compensation model on usage-based products to something more akin to "You get paid when the customer regularly uses the thing and Podium gets paid." Boom. Better performance all around.

Wisdom literature takeaway:

Focus on the inputs, and the outputs will follow.

But you get what you measure, not necessarily the output that follows from it.

Far vs. Fast

Bill Gates once said, "My success, part of it certainly, is that I have focused in on a few things," but if you don't trust Bill, we can take inspiration from Ron Swanson instead:

"Never half-ass two things; whole-ass one thing."

A big part of being a leader, rather mundanely, is merely assigning staff to work. In fact, one could argue that allocating staff is *the most important part* of modern-day business decision-making.

How is the company mission and vision actually achieved? By making sure people are assigned to the right tasks and teams to achieve it. What is the primary method by which we set priorities when building and selling products? Assigning staff!

At its most simplistic, let's say I've got 100 engineers who can build software. I can have them work, each separately, on 100 different things, or I can have them work together, all 100, on a single thing. Or any combination in between. Do I whole-ass one thing? Do I half-ass 100 things? There's a time for each.

Inside of this most-important leadership activity of staff allocation, we find all manner of competing approaches. The previous quotes represent an entire school of business book thought that pushes "focus" above all else. Oooooh, business books love themselves some focus. The idea is simple: you figure out what's most important and then work on that. In terms of assigning staff, it means you put all your people on the thing you've settled on "whole-assing."

As a product leader in software, I get this push from above and below and from the side all the time. "John, are your people doing too much? Should we drop some priorities?"

It's a great push and often right! For example, when I joined Podium, the R&D team was building software across three broad dimensions.

- Deliver every product a local business needs to manage the relationship with their customer across communications, marketing, and payment.

- Support most verticals that operate locally, including home and professional services, retail, healthcare, and automotive.

- Support all sizes of local businesses all the way from "mom-and-pop" operations to multi-thousand-location enterprises.

As an added bonus, we were dogfooding our product even though we weren't a local business, so we had to worry about keeping ourselves happy to boot!

This approach was unfocused. We were serving too many products to too many masters. So we got focused! We tightened our customer definition so that our product platform play could be better tailored to the portion of the market we had the strongest right to win. And the way that we instantiated that change was by allocating staff away from non-core customer products and projects over to core customer work! Staff allocation is the chief way a leader enforces a strategy change.

Humorously, though, as much push as I've received to "focus," I've received just as much push to *not focus too much*.

Usually this push in technology centers around efficiency and the concept of the *mythical man-month*. The basic idea is that if you're trying to build a thing, then adding a bunch more staff to that thing is just going to slow the team down, not speed them up and make the product better.

Jeff Bezos once said of building teams, "We try to create teams that are no larger than can be fed by two pizzas," said Bezos. "We call that the two-pizza team rule."

By that measure, I could probably be a team all unto myself, but maybe I'm just super hungry as I sit in the coffee shop writing this when the only thing under glass in here is a bran muffin and some kind of gluten-free pastry.

As a team increases in size, the number of person-to-person connection points increases *geometrically* with the size of that team. On an 8-person team, you've got 28 possible connections (think of them as one-to-one Slack conversations) between employees. Double that team to 16 folks, and 28 jumps to 120 one-to-one connections! And it only gets worse from there.

That means communication and collaboration break down fast as a team increases in size. You have to put in more *processes* to handle the team size. You have to hire "meta" roles like product, project, and program managers (the three horsemen of the process apocalypse).

So in a desire to focus, you might try putting everyone on a singular priority. But now instead of getting two "unfocused" things, you're going to get one thing, and you're going to get it *slower than you otherwise would have gotten it in the first place!* Everyone is too busy figuring out how to work together to get their newly focused shit done.

So what do you do? Break up the teams into smaller teams with disjoint priorities so they can move fast, of course! But wait, isn't that where we started?

It's a contradictory tightrope. Leaders must choose between having too few and too many priorities for their staff allocations. Too many priorities, and you're too unfocused to win your most important battles. Too many staff assigned to any single priority, and you might just get stuck.

OK then. Let's bastardize one of those unattributable apocryphal proverbs for our next **wisdom literature takeaway:**

If you want to go fast, go alone; if you want to go far, go together.

But if you "go together" too much, you won't get very far because you can't figure out how to move together well. Maybe go alone after all.

Process

The flip side of people is process. As a leader, you have to decide not only who to hire, how many, what they should work on, how to pay them, etc., but you also need to make decisions around *how will everyone work together?* And if there's an area of the business with more contradictions than People, it's Process. Because if a human being is weird and complex (I mean. . .we eat egg salad for fun. Doesn't get weirder than that.), then how two humans relate is complexity-squared!

Speed vs. Order

Some years ago, Facebook's much criticized motto was "Move fast and break things." Progress over perfection, over privacy, and over a whole host of other concerns was lauded.

Of course, then Facebook stepped in controversy after controversy. They acquired a legal team large enough to fill a Carnival cruise ship, and moving fast to build the product ceased to be possible.

Folks inside and outside the company criticized the mantra. You often heard the opposite mantra used in tech: "Move slow and fix things." Oooooh, engineers liked that one! Burn down tech debt. Fix bugs. The "'Re's' of the Product Apocalypse" were unleashed: "Replatform, refactor, rearchitect." Stop shipping brittle code. Stop taking that experimental product from last week's hackathon and releasing it to all the customers as if it were fully baked.

So which is it?

I've seen both work well!

At Podium, we've released some products that haven't worked out well from time to time. The product ends up clunky and underused. And yet I'll see the product team approach changing that failing product with a great deal of "big company" thinking. Folks often assume that it's more professional to proceed with caution. Got a product that's got like 10 customers on it and it's not working well? Welp, let's execute a bunch of research, write a big ol' doc, create unending design explorations, pull in every team we can think of, and create the perfect iteration on our next go.

Why waste the time!? When your product is terribly unpopular, then you needn't worry about angering the approximately zero happy customers using it. And what are the odds you can do worse as you alter it? If you're serving up day-old cold cheddar and broccoli soup, most people would be happy to just try whatever else you got. So haul ass! Move fast. Break things. Because the things you'd break suck anyway.

But what if the product you're working on is exceptionally popular or if it's critical infrastructure for your customers? Well, then it's not cold soup. At Mailchimp we rarely changed the email builder. Why? Because we had millions of users on it! It was responsible for the more than two billion emails we'd send daily. Small changes resulted in massive swings to one of our core values for customers. We moved slowly and fixed things.

Wisdom literature takeaway:

Move fast and break things except when you can't.

And then move slow and fix things.

There's probably a time when you should just go somewhere between fast and slow too . . .

Specialization vs. Generalization

"All trades, arts, and handiwork have gained by division of labor, namely, when, instead of one man doing everything, each confines himself to a certain kind of work distinct from others in the treatment it requires, so as to be able to perform it with greater facility and in the greatest perfection."

—Immanuel Kant

Nothing is more dangerous than relying on me, a product leader, to perform customer research. I couldn't be more self-deluded about "what the customer wants." My version of a customer interview is merely an exercise in leading the witness. *So tell me, why is that feature I just showed you the most awesome idea humankind has ever had?*

When I led Product at Mailchimp, I'd see this same delusional behavior from many of my product managers. And the same went not only for qualitative research but for quantitative as well. Product managers would spot the trends that favored their product, and that's the data they'd report on. Anything that might disagree with their gut was minimized (often subconsciously). It's not all bad; you want a product leader who's rooting for their product!

That said, allowing the product managers to roll their own research can lead to an unhealthy situation that one of my peers once dubbed, "It's always sunny in product-land."

You end up with folks who have one set of skills (vision-setting and prioritization) bringing a dangerous combination of ineptitude and over-confidence to a foreign practice (e.g., research), which ends up leading teams astray.

So how did we solve this at Mailchimp? Specialization!

We hired UX researchers who handled our customer interviews, surveys, and usability tests. And for quantitative work, we created a product analytics team.

Suddenly we were interrogating our customers and our own data in ways that made more sense. We'd get research back that ran counter to the narrative that all was sunny in product-land. There were some dark clouds!

Throughout any business, we can see the positive effects of specialization. At Podium, our best salesfolk are not terribly good at customer service. Our accountants are excellent at accounting, but they're not necessarily skilled in pricing and packaging. A leader needs to be able to identify when a particular task at a company requires and benefits from specialists. And yet. . .

"Overspecialization can lead to collective tragedy even when every individual separately takes the most reasonable course of action."

—David Epstein, Range: Why Generalists Triumph in a
Specialized World

After a time at Mailchimp, our specialist approach to researching and building products began to experience what I dubbed "the dream problem."

Our dreams are interesting only to ourselves. Being sued in a court of law by a chicken nugget is interesting. Showing up naked to a college math exam as a 40-year-old is interesting.

But how many of us *actually enjoy listening to our friends and family recount their dreams?*

Most dreams are weird, so whenever I try to tell my wife about some strange dream I've had the night before, I'll often see her eyes glaze over. It's interesting to me because I dreamed it, but not necessarily to anyone else. Surreal half-narratives make for boring breakfast conversations. "Cool story, bro."

I began to see the same thing at Mailchimp. A qualitative researcher would conduct a set of interviews, and then they'd present them to the team, but no one seemed to pay much heed to the findings. Why? Those interviews were the researcher's dream, no one else's! They hadn't been present for the customer conversation, so it lost its *visceral nature*; the customers didn't feel real.

So now we had better research, but *no one seemed to care as much about acting on it as when they'd conducted it themselves.*

In every function and in every business, specialization inherently creates barriers. To do my thing really intensely and with high quality, I have to focus on it. And that means *not focusing on your thing.*

This results in **"throwing it over the wall,"** a situation in which a specialist does their specific job, finishes, and throws the result over a wall to the next specialist to pick up.

The classic (and humorously celebrated) example of throw-it-over-the-wall behavior is Angostura bitters. Angostura bitters are a cocktail mainstay; the old fashioned, the Manhattan, the whiskey sour, even the mint julep will often call for Angostura as an ingredient or garnish.

So these bottles of bitters are everywhere across the world. But they're funny-looking! Specifically, the label is too big for the bottle. Where the bottle tapers toward the top, the label just keeps going.

As the story goes, the Seigert brothers who owned Angostura in the late 1800s divided their labor. One brother was responsible for making bottles. The other for making the labels. They both did their jobs just fine! And yet when they popped the labels on the bottles, they realized they'd made the labels too big for the bottles. Specialization had bred failure. But in a cute way. So they decided to roll with it.

At Podium, I wish I could say that the problems with specialization we've encountered were so cute, but alas, no. On the product side, where I've landed is that product managers are responsible for their own qualitative research and basic quantitative analysis. But analysts are available to consult on more complex quant work. I find that this keeps the product managers highly engaged with customers if not a little biased by their own visions for their products. And we use other mechanisms (specifically KPI reviews with myself and other executives) to ensure that teams are remaining honest and aren't straying too far off course due to the inherent bias injected by rolling their own findings.

But on the go-to-market side, we can't allow generalization. For sales staff to make the phone calls and close the deals they need each day, they don't have the time to onboard customers. And if we were to ask them to do that onboarding, a good closer wouldn't necessarily have the technical skill, patience, and pastoral bedside manner necessary to do a good job; they want to get back to earning commissions! We've instead relied on a throw-it-over-the-wall process wherein an account is sold by sales and onboarded by the customer success team. There was a time, however, where that toss over the wall *took days*. Not good! So to ensure specialization would work, we had to spend a great deal of time on that wall tossing. Our solution in that case was not turning the specialists into generalists, but rather we created the processes we needed for a warm handoff from one specialist to the other. Sale done? Cool. Let me transfer you *immediately* to your onboarder.

Once again then, we arrive at workable opposites. In my own day-to-day, I see examples of specialization and generalization operating better than the alternative, *depending on the context.*

Wisdom literature takeaway:

In a world of specialists, the generalist is king,

Except when you need them to do one thing super well, then they kind of suck.

So I guess specialists are kings too.

Top Down vs. Bottom Up

"Those closest to the pain should be closest to the power."
—Ayanna Pressley

"If I had asked people what they wanted, they would have said faster horses."
—Henry Ford (There's no evidence he actually said this, but if he's cool, I'm cool, right, Henry?)

In the 1990s, many retailers learned that kids have a lot of buying power. Companies started advertising more directly to children than ever before. They'd buy space on Saturday morning television; channels like Nickelodeon gave them ample opportunities to shill products all day long. It was the Golden Era of Nerf.

And one of the most popular tactics these ads would employ would be to appeal to some version of, "Parents just don't get it." Parents are out of touch. They make you clean your room and eat broccoli. Hit a dad in the nuts on TV with a Nerf dart, and you could strike advertising gold.

I find myself, as a product leader, feeling more and more like someone people want to shoot in the nuts with a Nerf gun. Oftentimes, deservedly. The main criticism I receive from folks is that I'm too "dictatorial" and too "top down" for how far I am from customers, their problems, and the products we build to solve those problems. *John just doesn't understand.*

It's fair. As the previous quote indicates, those closest to pain (customer problems in the context of business) should have the decision-making power! If not "the customer is always right," then at least "those interacting with the customers are always right."

I am the most dangerous type of leader: I have lots of ideas, lots of confidence, and a natural ability to describe and argue for those ideas clearly despite being *absolutely wrong 50 percent of the time.* My best product leaders are the ones who are very comfortable telling me, "Our customers would hate that. You're an idiot."

You can always tell when a product was designed in a boardroom. Customers weren't asking for a Microsoft version of the iPod. But we got the Zune. Customers weren't asking for a paid version of YouTube with high-production-value shorts. But we got Quibi. Y'all remember the ESPN phone? Facebook Home? The Fire Phone? Those were arguably born from top-down corporate copycatting, not from the bottom up.

So, "parents just don't understand," and we should let teams close to the customer make decisions. Yes? I've certainly benefited from this approach! At Podium, one of our products is a VoIP phone system for local businesses. And while we were building it, I was dictatorial in some ways. I demanded that we offer a full hardware phone system. That's what local businesses had on site, and I assumed they wouldn't be ready to make the jump to a purely software-based phone solution.

But then the team building the offering kept talking to customers. They did an alpha and a beta, and lo and behold, John *just didn't understand.* Tons of our customers were ready to ditch hardware (if they hadn't already). They wanted software-based phones without any hardware, and they wanted them now! It became our number-one product road-map priority.

Had I allowed the team to lead from the ground up, it's possible we would've saved time and effort getting to a solution that customers wanted faster.

So what's the catch?

I call it "Current Customer Stockholm Syndrome." And I see it most from leaders who used to work in customer support, which makes sense.

Essentially, Current Customer Stockholm Syndrome is the "faster horses" conundrum Henry Ford apocryphally referenced. Current customers tend to want more of what they bought *a while ago* when they purchased whatever it is they purchased from you. But they're not necessarily interested in a company's innovations, especially new products rather than innovations on current products.

At Mailchimp, every time we released a new email newsletter editor to existing customers, they'd all lose their collective minds. We just moved millions of people's cheese. The new editor was always tested and proven to make life easier for folks, but existing customers had muscle memory they'd built over time that made the existing editor *feel easier* even if it was old and kludgy. So every time we would release a new editor, we'd receive *a flood* of negative feedback from existing users (often power users and our best customers) yelling, "Why'd you mess up my workflow?"

The product leaders who were *closest to the customer* would feel this feedback most acutely. Their reaction would be, "Roll it back! The new editor is bad!"

The problem here is that releasing products merely for existing customers, particularly power users, is a search for a "local optimum," which is to say a product that's great for a type of existing customer and terrible for the rest, **in particular for future customers**. This is a specific case of the "innovator's dilemma" wherein existing customers suck all the oxygen from the room as it were.

The folks who are closest to the customer are often held hostage by current customer feedback, which makes them blind to the strategic, future-facing problems of the business. Sure, our existing customers love this old email editor. But to our new customers (and to the larger noncustomer public), the old email editor makes no sense!

Existing customers are usually customers you brought on *in the past*, which means being close to the current customer inherently makes you a student of the company *you once were* and not the company you wish *to become*. This means the problems you care about are those of existing product quality (fixing errors in existing products, making little tweaks) rather than making evolutionary jumps.

Existing BlackBerry customers weren't asking for touchscreens, integration into an MP3-purchasing ecosystem, better games, etc. They were interested in stuff like. . .business security. And yet, Apple destroyed BlackBerry in the early 2000s not by serving existing BlackBerry users but by articulating a whole new vision of a smartphone, its integrated value, and its primary user. It was a vision that not only expanded the smartphone market but pulled over the existing BlackBerry customer into a future Apple created.

So serving existing customers, and, in particular, giving them what they're asking for again and again and again, is merely abdicating leadership responsibilities to the mob. And while existing customers know what *they want*, they have no idea what the larger addressable market wants (that's of no interest to them) nor are they even representative of such a market.

And so we're left with a contradiction: sometimes it's best to go bottom up, i.e., to yield decision-making authority to those closest to the problem and to the customer. However, sometimes yielding to the voice of the customer is a race to the past, not to the future.

Wisdom literature takeaway:

Let those closest to the customer have the authority to make a decision,

Except when your customer might not be representative of where the market or your company is headed,

Then closeness to the current customer might limit your future options.

Product

The third broad category of decisions you may have to make as a leader (depending on your role) is product (I'm counting services in this broad category). I'm a product leader, so I'm biased, but this is what business is all about: selling *something* to customers. But how do you decide what to build, how good it'll be, and how to price it? Companies make myriad product decisions as they produce and take their offering to market.

There's no one right way to build a product and bring it to market, though. A Mercedes is very different from a Taco Bell Chalupa. On the spectrum of quality, they occupy different spaces. They're positioned from a marketing perspective totally differently. Does that make one of these products more right or more wrong? No! I bet eating a Taco Bell Chalupa inside a Mercedes is probably a nice way to spend 15 minutes.

Let's explore some options as you think about your own product or service.

Good vs. Great

"Mark seven times and cut once."
> —Benvenuto Cellini, 1560, citing a common aphorism

"Perfect is the enemy of good."
> —Voltaire, 1770, citing a common aphorism

I work in business-to-business (B2B) software as a service (SaaS). It's one of the most forgiving industries in terms of product quality. If you've ever had to use Salesforce, you're well aware of just how forgiving businesses can be with respect to quality; Salesforce may be one of the most successful businesses of all time, but its product is an experiential dumpster fire.

SaaS software doesn't need to get much right when it releases stuff because after all, we don't distribute software on disks anymore. If my internet application has a bug in it, we just fix the engine while the plane is flying! That's a lot different than needing to do a recall on an automobile or a pound of ground beef.

And yet even in SaaS, we debate the question constantly, "How good is good enough? How good is over-built?" If we all lived forever and if money didn't matter, we'd all want our work to be perfect. But there's a cost to perfection, both real (person hours spent building something, materials, etc.) and opportunity (we could've been doing something else!). So, do you spend the time making something just right, or do you just roll out with "good enough for government work"?

I once built a product where the head of marketing dug their heels in hard on quality. They would not market the product I was building until it met certain quality standards. Specifically, the product had to work well *worldwide* before we took it to market and tested its economic viability. They were uninterested in a version of the product that worked in the United States only. Internationalization took us more than a year to build. Finally, we got there and rolled it out, and the head of marketing marketed it.

The product was not terribly successful. It *worked* worldwide, and it was a failure worldwide. It was the *John Carter* of software when we were hoping for a *John Wick*.

We'd taken the time to measure "seven times." We'd made sure the product was so technically buttoned up that you could use it anywhere from Cape Town to Stockholm to Manitoba, needlessly so as it turns out. Because no one wanted to buy it anyway.

My product manager on the product was pissed! And this was a guy who never got flustered. But this situation angered him like none before.

He came into my office sometime after our not-so-successful launch and said, "Remember how I wanted to build a stripped-down version of the product for the U.S. market that would've taken about two months to build? We could've failed fast and avoided this situation."

He was right. I'd caved to my peer in marketing, and it'd cost me and the company big. We polished a turd for an extra 10 months. What a waste.

Well, I learned my lesson there and started pushing things out early and often. I'd "ready, fire, aim" like none other after that. Market testing "minimum viable products" became the name of the game.

Of course, that led to self-fulfilling prophecies; I'd release dogshit (from a product quality perspective), and when customers didn't like it, well, now I didn't know if it was because the idea was flawed or the execution was just so bad as to make a good idea unpalatable.

That's what happened when we tested early versions of the Podium phone system. It became apparent that 100 percent uptime was the expectation. Problems, even problems that weren't our fault (like a customer's Wi-Fi going down), wouldn't be tolerated when it came to call quality.

Context matters a lot when dealing in quality. Are you competing in a "red ocean" where the waters are already filled with competitors thrashing about? Are you releasing a novel product where customer expectations are low? Is your product an essential utility that has to work 100 percent of the time (like phone and internet service), or can it be a little flaky? Flakiness can even be permitted along certain dimensions and not others. For example, Tesla has concentrated on its software and technology, its battery, its network of charging stations, its drivetrain, while shipping flaky bodies with poor construction, and customers have been tolerant of this, because the novelty has nothing to do with whether the door is perfectly flush when closed.

Wisdom literature takeaway:

Ship a great product if you can,

Unless that's going to take too long and be too expensive, and you're not even certain if people want it.

Then ship an OK product, but if OK isn't going to cut it with customers,

Uh, then ship a great product I guess.

Bundling vs. Unbundling

"[There are] only two ways to make money in business: one is to bundle; the other is unbundle."

—Jim Barksdale

When Podium started, it was a single product with a single focus: get more Google and Facebook reviews for local businesses. And it did this with SMS. Send a customer an SMS message after they receive their product or service and say, "Hey! Leave us a review!" and add a link to click to submit the review. It was a simple idea. And it worked great! Local businesses had been relying on customers to leave reviews completely of their own volition prior to that, and guess who most often left a review? The pissed people!

Podium changed that.

But once this product was on the market and local businesses were snatching it up, what was the company to do next? There was a fork in the road.

One path was to "bundle." Podium had a product that communicated with customers over SMS. Maybe there would be other SMS products we could sell to local businesses, like collecting payment, collecting and talking to inbound leads from the website, and so on. We could transform into an entire front-office management solution for local business! All communication, all payment, all marketing! All in one!

The other path was to stay "unbundled" and simply double down on the product we had. This meant becoming exclusively an expert in what's known as "reputation management." Build features for responding to customer reviews, support more sites like Yelp, Cars.com, or Angie's List, etc. There was a lot to do in the space, and as we made the product better and better, we could sell to the gamut of local businesses from mom-and-pop shops to large local enterprises with thousands of locations or branches.

The business world is full of winners and losers based solely on whether they took their product in a bundled or unbundled direction.

Apple bundled up a camera, a GPS navigation system, an MP3 player, a work computer, a flashlight, and more with its phone. Clearly that paid off. Netflix, on the other hand, unbundled access to content from the cable package. That paid off too!

On the other hand, when Amazon decided to bundle itself with hardware in the form of the Fire phone (or even Alexa), customers were not terribly receptive. And when Google unbundled Internet (Google fiber) from the standard telco offering (Internet, phone, TV), while many customers were on board, the real-world (political, infrastructure, etc.) investment needed to unbundle Internet away from the telcos made the move problematic, and it stalled out around 2016 and has hobbled along ever since.

At Podium, we decided to bundle up. We built out a full communications suite (phones, SMS, social messaging), payments (including reader hardware, payments over text, lending, and more), and marketing tools. All the products work together using a customer relationship management (CRM) solution at the center.

We felt our relationships with our customers would allow us to expand them into other products beyond reviews. The gamble paid off, and now our most successful customers are using us for three or more products at a time. To make it all work, though, we had to transition our go-to-market machine from a "one-bite-at-the-apple" sales machine (sell review collection and move on) to an expansion machine (sell reviews, then lead collection, texting, phones, payments, and so on).

This move opened up the total addressable market for Podium, but it was not without its drawbacks. Our enterprise customers weren't necessarily interested in our integrated solution because they had very specific needs for some of the products (for example, they needed a phone system that could operate a customer support call center with hundreds of folks in it; that's hardly "local business"). Instead, our largest customers wanted us to focus solely on review collection and make it a Swiss Army knife of reputation management. With limited resources, we were unable to do that, and some of our enterprise customers were left unhappy.

The decision to bundle up offerings to make an attractive package or to peel a single product off from somewhere it has been bundled before and do it better, once again (you're getting the pattern), is contextual. Both routes can lead to riches or to abject failure.

Wisdom literature takeaway:

Bundle up multiple products to create something of value for customers,

Or peel something out of a bundle that already exists and just do that singular thing super well.

Build vs. Buy

"If you want a thing done well, do it yourself."
—often credited to Napoleon Bonaparte, but we all know it was probably your dad who said it first

"If you think it's expensive to hire a professional to do the job, wait until you hire an amateur."
—Red Adair

I once was running late for a dinner party where I was supposed to bring a side dish. There was no time to cook, so I grabbed a casserole dish with a lid and ran out the door. My next stop was Popeyes, America's best restaurant (don't fight me on this). I bought a bunch of orders of red beans and rice. In the parking lot, I dumped them in my casserole dish and popped the lid on top. I disposed of the evidence discretely.

At the dinner party, my side dish was a hit.

"These beans are so creamy!" Damn right they were; they're Popeyes' beans.

"Can I get the recipe?" someone asked. I texted them a Google Maps pin to Popeyes.

In the case of red beans and rice, for me, when I want something done, well, I hire a professional.

In business, one is constantly faced with whether to home-cook a meal or just buy it from a drive-thru.

At Mailchimp, there was a piece of our infrastructure for sending billions of emails that we had bought from another company. Well, technically we rented; we were paying annual license fees. It was a convenient enough arrangement. The vendor gave us pretty good pricing, and we didn't need to code up that piece of infrastructure ourselves.

Then one year the vendor increased the cost. Not by 10 or 20 percent. No, they increased by a factor of five. They were trying to bleed us. Luckily, we had a price currently locked in for a number of months before our contract expired. And we realized we had the internal talent necessary to build the infrastructure ourselves! So we pulled together some folks and built our own capability to replace that piece that we'd rented for so long. At one price, it made sense to rent. Once that price went through the roof, though, paying some engineers to own instead of rent, well, that became a no-brainer. Buying used to be the best option, right up until it wasn't.

On the flip side, my background is in data science, so when it comes to machine learning, I'm always a "If you want it done right, do it yourself" kind of guy. That is, until I started playing around with GPT3, ChatGPT, and all sorts of third-party machine learning models Podium could tap into via API. No need to productionalize models yourself. I desperately wanted to find a reason to make all of Podium's machine learning capabilities homegrown, but it no longer made much sense. I mothballed my graduate degree and started buying.

Companies and teams often have competencies in one of these two approaches. Salesforce is a growth-by-acquisition machine. Apple has a knack for rolling its own everything. And there are advantages either way. Acquiring can give you access to a market immediately, talent you don't have, and technology that could take years to build. Building something yourself provides you a chance to control the customer experience better and integrate better with your other systems or products.

Too often this debate becomes seemingly religious in nature. Those who value the craft of something will push for home-growing it, like me with data science. Those who run corporate development departments will see every opportunity through a buy lens. That's the only tool they have, and to a hammer, it's all nails, baby!

Both ways are right and wrong. Once again, it's all about context.

Wisdom literature takeaway:

If you want to do something right, do it yourself,

Except when someone else can do it more "right" than you; then just buy that shit.

I Didn't Give You Answers; I Gave You Options

I'm going to stop there, but consider this chapter as a resource: one of many places to go to for options. I'm going to collect these 10 sections "Proverbs-style right here for you:

Business wisdom stands at the high point of the city.

From its Ted Talk it calls, "Let all who have ears, look up from your phones and heed my cries."

Hire A players.

Except when B players do better in the role.

Then B is A. So I guess still hire A players. But like B-ish A players.

Run a blameless culture so that people will take more risks.

Run a high-accountability culture so that people will make more impact.

Focus on the inputs, and the outputs will follow.

But you get what you measure, not necessarily the output that follows from it.

If you want to go fast, go alone; if you want to go far, go together.

But if you "go together" too much, you won't get very far because you can't figure out how to move together well. Maybe go alone after all.

Move fast and break things except when you can't.

And then move slow and fix things.

There's probably a time when you should just go somewhere between fast and slow too . . .

In a world of specialists, the generalist is king,

Except when you need them to do one thing super well, then they kind of suck.

So I guess specialists are kings too.

Let those closest to the customer have the authority to make a decision,

Except when your customer might not be representative of where the market or your company is headed,

Then closeness to the current customer might limit your future options.

Ship a great product if you can,

Unless that's going to take too long and be too expensive and you're not even certain if people want it.

Then ship an OK product, but if OK isn't going to cut it with customers,

Uh, then ship a great product I guess.

Bundle up multiple products to create something of value for customers,

Or peel something out of a bundle that already exists and just do that singular thing super well.

If you want to do something right, do it yourself,

Except when someone else can do it more "right" than you; then just buy that shit.

Now, I know that format is absolutely absurd, but this I hope illustrates how impossible it is to learn how to lead by book. For so many pieces of good advice (such good advice that they often come with aphorisms or famous quotes), the opposite is often just as defensible. Good advice means options, not answers! And deciding between a spectrum of options falls on you, the leader. We'll get into that a bit in Chapter 4.

Let's Do a Little Exercise

The trick at this point is to *get comfortable being uncomfortable*. Get comfortable with leadership having no clear answers that work every time. Context matters a lot! As an exercise in getting comfortable, I want you to grab a pen (for you audiobook listeners, go to shortenedlink.com/leadershipwise) and look at that chunk of 10 "wisdom" takeaways given earlier. For each takeaway, I want you to circle the option most in line with your personality. Circle your starting place, your "go-to."

If you're a craftsperson at heart, you likely love specialization, doing it yourself, and shipping a great product. I know a lot of engineers like that. If you're a little dictator (D on DISC, 8 on enneagram, ENTJ, etc.), you likely love high accountability and moving fast. Circle what feels most natural to you. You won't hurt my feelings by marking up my collection of beautiful poetry.

Now take 10 minutes and *think about the options you didn't circle*. Can you think of occasions you've encountered where in that context perhaps that option was the best way to go? This is you warming up. This is you becoming a less rigid, modern, dogmatic leader; you're beginning to think in an options-based way. You're wising up!

CHAPTER

3

Generating Options

To get the most out of this book, I'd love for you to take a moment and think of a problem or two you're experiencing at work where *you have to make a decision on which way to go*.

I've included in this book a worksheet where you can fill that problem in (**www.wiley.com/go/leadershipwise**).

It's OK if you don't have the most articulate definition of the decision you're trying to make just yet. No one is grading your work in this book, and we'll workshop what you've got as you go.

Now, the purpose of this chapter is to start generating options to solve that problem. Remember, the argument I'm making here is that *there's never one right answer to all situations*, so looking at options and choosing rightly between them is the primary mark of a good leader. Now it's time to start flexing those options-generating muscles!

In Chapter 2, we took a walk around the business and discussed the often contradicting options for solving some high-level categories of problems at a business. But now let's dive into the specifics of your problem.

To choose a solution to your problem, **you must have options**. The worst leaders I know are, like I talked about earlier in this book, are those leaders who think there's only one option ever to each decision point they encounter. These are the broken record leaders. They manage by business book, but the books they select are often just amplifiers of their own personality. If they're amped, they'll read *Amp It Up*. If they're ponderous, they'll read *Slow Down to Speed Up*.

I had a housemate once who was the slowest man I'd ever met. Watching him tie his shoes was a trip. He didn't do the whole "the fox goes round the tree and through the hole" thing. No, no, no. That was too fast for him! He'd painstakingly form two loops with his two laces. Then he'd tie those loops together into a knot. It was the most literal, most plodding way to tie laces into a bow that I'd ever seen!

In all things, just like his laces, he'd take the slow road. He'd rather talk on the phone than text. He drove under the speed limit everywhere. Whenever I heard his bedroom door open, I knew I had at least a full minute before I'd see him on the stairs, taking each step slowly and with care.

Well, one time this friend and I were talking, and he mentioned how challenged he'd felt by a quote he'd recently read from Dallas Willard. The quote goes as follows, "Hurry is the great enemy of the spiritual life in our day. You must ruthlessly eliminate hurry from your life."

It's an awesome quote. But I couldn't help but chuckle. Eliminate hurry! I thought to myself, you, my friend, have already eliminated the hurry; you need the opposite! May I interest you in a Red Bull?

But that's how *all* of us operate. We make decisions from a place of a singular option: the option that comes most naturally to us. And we spend our lives consuming advice and generating experiences that buttress that option; it's an echo chamber of our own making. Echo chambers are snuggly and warm, like bean-bags. But who ever had made a series of good decisions from a beanbag?

In this chapter, we're going to simply push against that by generating multiple options for our particular decision before we make it. So this chapter is broken into sections based on where you might go to create options. You can think about where you might source options as concentric rings around yourself, the owner of the decision.

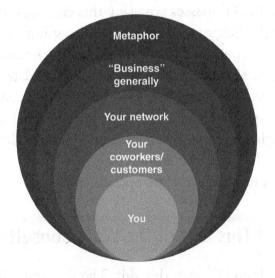

First you consult yourself for an option. Sometimes it can be hard to see beyond that first glaring option, so we clear the pipes straight away and then move beyond that. Next, you talk to others you work with, some who know the *context* (the customer, the business, the systems, or the affected parties) better than you. Then there's your network; you can talk to folks who do your job and make this particular decision, or you could talk to folks at other companies who serve the same customer, etc. After that, you enter the general realm of the business book. Lastly, perhaps least specific but most creatively generative, you enter the realm of "options by metaphor."

For the rest of this chapter, I'm going to generate options for a problem I currently face personally.

My decision problem: I've got a legacy product at Podium. It's called Team Chat. And I don't love it. Why? Because it's a bit off-strategy. I'm working with R&D to build out a *customer* interaction platform. But Team Chat doesn't interact with customers. Team Chat is basically a Slack/Teams competitor that's built into Podium itself. While employees at a local business are helping customers, they can also chat with each other. It's not fully off-strategy in that businesses are using this chat tool to coordinate how they help their customers (they're also using it to plan where to go to lunch), but would I prioritize building it today? Unlikely.

But we've already got the product as it predates my tenure, and its active usage is tied to tens of millions in revenue (which is a lot for a startup!). So. . .what do I do with it? Do I shut it down, keep the lights on (staff it somewhat), replace it with something more aligned, or iterate it into a thing that "fits?"

Let's get to sourcing some options.

Let's Get This Out of the Way: Consult Yourself

Welp, let's Jiminy Cricket this shit. The first thing to do here is to "let your conscience be your guide." Your knee-jerk reaction, your instinct, is not necessarily bad! Hell, you're a leader for a reason. You've got experience. You've got a brain. What does that devil on your shoulder say you should do? That's option 1.

Option 1: KTLO: In the case of Team Chat, my instincts say, "'Keep the lights on until we all die of old age." Classic Microsoft backward compatibility play here. It doesn't have the revenue churn implications of shutting it down, and I can keep zero full-time staff on the feature by just having folks jump over to it when there are bugs. It's stable enough that that's not all the time. Just keep it running, but that's all.

OK, that's my inclination, easily generated by mumbling to myself while I sip my coffee in traffic. The important thing here is to first **acknowledge the knee-jerk reaction**. And second, to acknowledge *why*. For my part, my inclination to ignore Team Chat as best I can (no fully staffed team to it, just ad hoc bug fixes) comes from my own experience. I don't like putting staff on nonstrategic priorities. When you fund and staff a thing (project, product, team, department, etc.), people find a way of "creating gravity," i.e., sucking in additional resources, additional attention, additional customers. This is why we're great at creating government agencies and terrible at killing them! So I don't like funding things off-strategy; I'd rather just keep this thing alive part-time. I'd kill it if I could, but it's tied to too much revenue. I think that people tend to overestimate the cost of keeping the lights on for something (although there are person-hour and context-switching costs for sure), and they underestimate the total impact of deprecating a product that's got some traction.

All right, I've got my first option! The one that's most natural to me and fits my experience the best. Let's pull some more.

Do you have yours? If so, fill it in the worksheet (**www .wiley.com/go/leadershipwise**).

Perhaps you've already got a couple variants, and you're a little divided between the two. That's OK! Write them both in. But list the one that's your *natural tendency* first just to force yourself into some self-awareness.

Consult Your Co-workers and Customers

As we discussed in Chapter 2, the folks closest to the problem are often (not always!) going to know best.

If this is a customer-facing problem, talk to customers! Prospects too. Do they understand the product? Does the marketing confuse them? Does your customer support make their heart leap like a gazelle to hear from you?

Don't stop there. Talk to the folks who talk to the customers day in and out. They'll be pulling from a larger sample of qualitative feedback.

If this isn't customer-facing, talk to those co-workers most affected by the decision. For example, if this is a staffing and performance decision, like maybe whether to fire someone, talk to those they work with internally. If it's a process problem, talk to the folks who will be impacted by a process change.

Now, as I said, being closest to the affected product, customer, employee, and so on doesn't make someone necessarily right all the time, but it sure does help to have a ton of context! The peers of someone you might fire might be too close to them relationally ("they're good people") to see that they're not meeting your expectations. The folks who'd be affected by a process change might be too entrenched in their muscle memories to see the value in a change. If you want to find out whether it's a good idea to raise sales quotas, well, the sales rep will have an opinion on that for sure, but it might not be highest value.

Now work your way out on the org chart from the epicenter.

Consult your peers, i.e., those at your level who operate in different functions. These folks see problems from a different angle and often *work with different tools*. What I see as a design problem my CTO might see as an infrastructure problem and my CMO might see as a customer nurture problem. So while

I might try to fix a product with Figma, my CTO might fix it with Elasticsearch and my CMO with Marketo.

Additionally, if you feel comfortable (and I hope you do), you can on occasion take the problem up the chain, i.e., ask folks higher in the company. They'll likely have less context than you, but they'll often have more experience or a broader view of the company and the market landscape that can generate options. For me that means chatting with my CEO. If you're a CEO, that might mean talking to a trusted board member, a cofounder, etc.

Set Expectations in These Conversations: You're Just Gathering Input

In all these directions (asking down, across, and up), you need to set expectations about what you're up to; options are not commitments. Sometimes when I ask a team below me for an option, they shit their pants because they think they'll be immediately committed to their answer.

"Here comes the whiplash!" Executives just don't understand. But if you are transparent about the problem you're facing and the options you're considering, you can lower a lot of blood pressure. I've found that when you're transparent with folks and treat them like adults, you can bring them further into a decision than most folks often do (more on that later in this book).

Sometimes when I ask a peer for an option, they see that as me trying to foist responsibility for a problem onto them. Sometimes when I escalate to my CEO, they see that as me trying to abdicate my responsibility. So think about who's best to talk to about your problem and always prepare them for the conversation. Preparing someone is easy:

"Hey, I'm trying to make a decision about the future of Team Chat, and I wanted to get your opinion. I'm not making a decision just yet; I'm in an information-gathering phase."

A little preamble is all it takes.

In my case, I consulted the team closest to the customers using Team Chat, and they definitely didn't see things my way.

Option 2: Fund it: "Keeping the lights on" requires the team to manage a codebase written years ago. They're fixing bugs that some dude named Kenneth wrote long before they even came to Podium. And they're sick of the context switching. They don't want to fix Team Chat bugs and then go back to their day job. At the same time, the folks closest to the customer see that everyone loves Team Chat. And they, unlike me, don't care *all that much that the product is off-vision* (this part hurts my feelings. . .I wish they cared more about my product vision, but I'll save the tears for when I'm alone on the commute home). Their recommendation is simple then: People are picking up what we're putting down, so we need to fund the product, modernize the code, and iterate.

Oh boy. Funding a product off-vision? I don't like that. But I store the option in my noggin' and let it marinate. Who knows, maybe the product vision is off.

I chat with sales, and they *love* this idea. Company and product vision be damned! They know how to sell this product, and they think more customers will buy it. But then again, I think, some customers bought the Pontiac Aztec; that doesn't mean it was the best product for Pontiac to produce. And our revenue data for Team Chat is middling at best. It's tied to some revenue, but it's not a star. More of a C-list actor honestly.

Then I walk down the hall to my colleague's office. He works in design, and he's worked at a ton of tech companies who've had similar problems. He's no closer to the customer than I am necessarily, but his experience and his design expertise give him a slightly different angle.

Option 3: Replace it with something on-vision: My colleague pointed out that while a Slack competitor doesn't help local businesses talk to customers, we could replace our Slack-like Team Chat with a tool that was more like Google Workspace's commenting system where local business employees could share and comment on customer profiles, customer conversations, and customer payments. By constraining Team Chat to make the employee conversations in Team Chat *about their customers*, we keep the popular product but bring it back to the CRM, which is what Podium is all about.

Good point! I'd love to replace this thing and migrate the current customers to something that fits the vision better. But is that the best use of our R&D resources? Feels pricey. I keep pulling in options.

Consult Your Network

So, when you're done consulting yourself and those you work with, whether below, across, or above, where to next? Your network is the place to start. Specifically, talk to folks who have at least one dimension of context with respect to your problem. Perhaps they do your job at another company (they understand the tools you can bring to bear), or perhaps they serve your same customer. Maybe they've been where you've been before.

I find it helpful to reach out to specific folks who I know will provide high-quality advice when solicited one on one. But if you're more of a Hail Mary, LinkedIn-for-all poster, have at it.

For this problem, I reached out to a couple other product executives who served the small business market, and I asked them how they've handled legacy products that were off-strategy but had traction. One of my buddies gave me a strong, unequivocal option.

Option 4: Kill it ("Revenue doesn't taste as good as having a skinny codebase feels"): My product contact made a very specific point for my problem. Sure, you've got some users on Team Chat, but is that all they're using from Podium? If they're using multiple products (since Podium is a multiproduct platform), a lot of them will probably stick around even if Team Chat were sunset. And if some folks are a little frustrated, offer them a discount! All that revenue that's at risk won't evaporate overnight. But do the homework on how important the product really is and think through customer save strategies. It's possible to minimize the impact.

This same person in my network also called my Keep the Lights On strategy "intellectually lazy and gutless." Ouch. Another thing to cry about on the commute.

Think through who you'd consult in your network. Do you have a mentor? Some previous co-workers you trust? A good little group of folks you banter with on Twitter? A local meetup or happy hour?

If you don't have such a support system like this outside your company, get something! That external perspective will always provide an option or two that feels foreign to folks inside the company, because company cultures brainwash (I mean that in the best possible way) people to "That's just how we do business" as a helpful shortcut to repeatable performance.

If you're at a company that always builds things from scratch, it may take that outside voice to urge "Just buy it off the shelf." If you're a company that relies on sales, it may take that outside voice to urge for "product-led growth." You get the point.

Go Ahead, Read the Business Books!

We've come full circle! At the beginning of this book, I crapped all over business books. Well, here they are again.

Most management books are great at providing options *so long as you remember that those options aren't definitive*. And those options are inherently distant from your context seeing as how a book is literally dead as in dead trees; the book doesn't know your customers, your business, your tools. But in many instances the author has encountered *similar situations*. So take what you can. They may be smarter than you (in my case, I assure you I'm not), but the author knows but a fraction of what you know about your *specific decision*.

In my case, I ended up picking up and flipping through a book I had on my shelf about the partnership economy, and the ideas in the book made me ask the question, "Can I solve Team Chat via a partnership?"

Option 5: Swap with an embedded partner: The idea is simple enough. Can we replace Team Chat by somehow framing in a white label chat product that exists outside the company? We'd pay a partner to white label the product, and we'd pop it in. Existing customers could be moved over without them necessarily even knowing. This option is a compromise. It keeps the off-vision feature around (at minimum for those using it), but the maintenance then shifts away from R&D and to business development in large part. This option isn't without costs! We'd still have to deprecate the current product, frame in the white labeled version, etc., but after some pain, it'd provide a lower investment going forward.

Management by Metaphor

Humans experience the world as a narrative. We love stories. We want to be grabbed by a story, by the characters, the rise and fall of action. Stories create empathy and emotion, they release chemicals in our brain like oxytocin, and they help us feel connected to reality and to purpose.

Often, the problems we experience feel *dry*. They feel disembodied and cold. And that actually prevents us from fully engaging some of the most *creative and generative* parts of our brain in creating options. By embedding the problem inside a story, even analogously, we're able to generate additional options. Seems silly, but it's true!

I can ask "What should I do about Team Chat?" in a vacuum. Dry. I can review the revenue data, the monthly active users, and the use cases that are attracting our customers to the tool, and that'll help a bit. In terms of dryness, it'll take the problem from saltines-level dryness to chicken breast–level dryness.

But the moment I interview a customer who uses Team Chat, *especially* if I interview a customer *inside their own physical space*, I'm placed into a specific story, different parts of my brain are activated, emotions are turned on, and (boom!) additional options come to light. Are they right necessarily? Nah. But they might be! They're options!

This is what makes very specific qualitative data, like customer interviews, so crucial. But it's not the only way to access these same parts of our brain when thinking through options. There is a crude shortcut to generate these narrative-based options, and that's to use simile or metaphor. I don't necessarily need a story about Team Chat. I need a story about *anything* that involves conflict and decision-making, and then I can metaphorically *connect it to my problem*.

This is why idioms even exist!

When someone says, "We need to cross the Rubicon!" or "We need to burn the boats!" they're using idioms that are actually small stories or small visuals from another situation altogether to generate and support an option. Folks pull these idioms from *everywhere*, most often from places that are full of visceral, emotional experience: sports, war, health, food, and religion to name a few.

Sports idioms:

- Blocking and tackling
- The score takes care of itself
- Best defense is a good offense
- Slow and steady wins the race

War idioms:

- Going scorched-earth
- Flank the competition
- Crossing the Rubicon

Food idioms:

- Meat and potatoes
- Eat our vegetables
- We have bigger fish to fry
- Have your cake and eat it too

Health idioms:

- We need to take our vitamins
- Take a temperature
- Stop the bleeding

Religious idioms:

- Robbing Peter to pay Paul
- Cut the baby in half
- Better the devil you know

We pull idioms from categories such as these *specifically because they trigger an emotional or visual reaction*. What's interesting is that it's for this exact same reason that such sayings are increasingly going out of style. *They're triggering.* "Cut the baby in half" is offensive! It's horrifying. That's what makes it such a visual and emotional metaphor for generating options to your dry problem.

But let's move beyond the obvious. Options can come from *any media we consume that we can relate to our decisions.* The key thing is that the media **grabs you** so that you can remember it and use it to help characterize situations in your life.

I recently watched the film *Bullet Train*, and in the movie, one of the hitmen uses *Thomas the Tank Engine*, its characters, and its stories to characterize the world around him and solve problems. Once he knows whether a person is a Thomas, a Percy, a Diesel, etc., then he knows how to handle them. The important thing for the assassin was that *Thomas the Tank Engine* grabbed him and filled his head with a grid for understanding the world around him.

For me, so often options come from movies and TV. When executives in tech proudly tell me of their ascetic lifestyles (they drink Soylent, they always dress the same way, they "don't own a TV," they mostly consume tech podcasts) because they think that this monklike lack of consumption outside tech will lead them to leadership enlightenment, I have to laugh. It's precisely the stuff I consume outside tech that leads me to be a better leader!

When I think about options that won't disrupt the momentum of the business, I compare them to Indiana Jones hot-swapping an idol with a bag of sand.

I learned about sunk costs from the film *Heat* where Val Kilmer kills two armored guards because he'd already acquired a life sentence from the murder of a previous armored guard.

I learned about "slowing down" AI magic in software user interfaces from *The Prestige* where Christian Bale's magical teleportation act happens too fast with too little fanfare for customers to understand they just paid for something extraordinary.

I learned to not obsess about tools but instead think about the problem itself from *Sneakers* where Robert Redford defeats an electronic keypad on a door lock, not by hacking it but simply by kicking the door in (the actual problem was the door, not the technology).

Reader, if there's one thing I commend you to do in this book, it's to not feel guilty about your consumption of whatever gives you a "metaphorical vocabulary" to generate options for leadership. For you that might be *Gilmore Girls* reruns or reality TV or sports or documentaries or eating bad food or going to Catholic Mass or reading biographies. Everything in moderation, of course, but humans are **cross-disciplinary pattern matchers**.

Lavoisier once said, "Nothing is lost, nothing is created, everything is transformed."

Or as the Britpop band Blur put it:

Nothing is wasted, only reproduced.

You see, everything we consume is raw material for creating options. Therefore, consume *memorable variety*, and by memorable, I mean media that hits your emotions; that's the good stuff. That'll be different for different people, and that's OK. And that's why we shouldn't shit on other people's interests as leaders; those interests are what generate option-diversity, otherwise known as the oft-lauded "diversity of thought."

The French came up with a literary term called *bricolage* that I think applies directly to leadership in business.

Bricolage is the concept of constructing art from stuff that *already exists*. Behind it is this idea that nothing is new; when we make decisions, when we make products, when we make food, etc., we're merely recombining things that have come before in new and interesting ways.

The same goes for business. We as leaders take in narratives, decisions, and paths others have taken, literally and metaphorically, every day. And then when it comes time to make our own decisions, it's our memories of these past narratives that turn us into the "bricoleur," i.e., a person who brings these past tales to bear on our current problem to generate (parts of) options from which to choose.

Hell, business books take this tactic *all the time*. The "swoop and poop" books I mentioned in Chapter 1 are perfect for this; their whole tactic is to pull in stories from Afghanistan, from K2, from the open ocean, from whatever adventure the author can relate to business. They're metaphor machines packed dubiously as answers, but they make for great options!

For me, the metaphorical option I ended up generating for my Team Chat problem came from Brussels sprouts of all things.

As a child, I remember Brussels sprouts being reviled almost universally. They were the stuff of Saturday morning cartoons right up there with lima beans and liverwurst. They were fart balls of bitter sadness.

Ross on *Friends* once called Brussels sprouts "worse than no food at all."

And then, 20 years later, Brussels sprouts started appearing all over menus! The coolest of menus in your town or city. They were cool somehow, and when I tasted them, I, like many folks, thought they tasted awesome. Had human taste buds changed? No! The Brussels sprout had changed, and as it turns out, it had *been intentionally changed* at a genetic level.

A Dutch scientist named Hans van Doorn had figured out what made these little green balls taste so bad *at a chemical level*.

And through crossbreeding modern Brussels with heirloom varieties, scientists were able to, more or less, *evolve* the sprout into a thing that didn't taste like a fart ball.

This story was bouncing around in my head one afternoon when I thought about Team Chat.

Option 6: Evolve it into a customer-centric system: The problem with option 3, i.e., replacing Team Chat with something on-vision, is that in 2022, we had users send millions of messages over Team Chat. So, a straight replacement (à la Indiana Jones swapping the idol for a bag of sand) was going to be fraught. For some time we'd operate two codebases, the old and the new, while we got the new product to MVP, and then we'd over time have to move users onto the new system. And if that system resembled Google Workspace's commenting system more than Slack, would they want to move? There was a risk that we'd end up KTLO-ing the old Team Chat while operating a newer Team Chat in tandem. Yuck.

Evolution then was an option. Staff a Team Chat team fully and ask them to produce a road map that slowly evolves the Team Chat feature into something that supports a customer communication platform. They'll need to learn the old codebase just like in the KTLO option, but their work won't be as soul-crushing because they'll be slowly altering and constraining the feature to support only those "chats" that were in line with Podium's purpose (conversations would be about customer conversations, payments, reviews, appointments, etc., rather than about where the office might eat lunch that day). If done right, we could still permit the occasional lunch discussion too.

A Little Note on Diversity

Companies have been taking more steps than ever to hire a diverse employee base. And you can give (and academics have) a number of reasons why this is important. I want to take a moment in the context of this chapter to underscore its importance.

When creating options for decisions, a primary source for options (as discussed) as well as your chief sounding board is your colleagues, whether we're talking about those under you, to the left of you, or over you. You want these colleagues to provide differing perspectives, i.e., to literally suggest options you wouldn't think of on your own. Company culture seeks to iron out variety to a degree by instilling the "company way," so it becomes extra important to make sure that folks entering the company are capable of providing so much variety in the way of options that they can survive some degree of *cultural smoothing*.

Diversity comes in many categories: age, gender, ethnicity, place, work experience, education experience, etc. Many factors shape an individual's experience of the world, and that means they all approach situations with different pattern matching abilities, different tools for solving problems, and hence different options-generating potential.

Let's take age as an example. Someone who worked through the dot-com bust or who worked through the Great Financial Crisis understands certain risks differently than those who weren't in the job market yet. Similarly, those who are older might be more familiar with "database marketing," whereas younger folks might speak the language of the "customer data platform." These experiences, differences in tools and vocabulary, and ultimately different ways of seeing the world can generate variety in the options we consider when charting a path forward.

The flip side is hiring a bunch of people who are all rather the same, ironing out what remaining uniqueness there might be with company enculturation, barely consulting them when making a decision (relying on that knee jerk instead), and using business books that agree with typical approaches rather than challenge them. That's a sadly common occurrence in business (even in rather progressive workplaces; sameness can look a lot of ways), and it leads to *local* maxima in decision-making at best and poor performance over the long haul.

What Are My Levers? Chart Options Against Your Decision Levers

We've collected a first round of options. I've got six of them already. None of them when taken at face value are *wrong* even though they go in contradictory directions (kill versus fund, for example).

When generating your options, one thing to think through is, "What levers do I have to pull?" Your options then are merely combinations of the levers and knobs you have at your disposal.

It's similar to looking in the pantry at what ingredients you have available when asking the question, "What can I whip up for dinner?"

In my case, I'm the chief product officer, and that quickly connotes a few levers. I can staff a team to work on a thing or not.

Indeed, the clearest lever I have to pull in my job is staffing. Another lever I have is that I own the product (and the product road map) globally for the company, so while Team Chat already exists, I can choose whether to Keep It or Kill It. I didn't bring you into this world, but I can take you out of it!

Another lever for me is the product vision, which I own. I can tolerate a product outside the vision (which in a way is incorporating it into the vision, i.e., doing a deal with the devil), or I can reject it. This lever is partially correlated with the other two. Something inside the vision must be staffed *eventually*. Something outside the vision must be deprecated *eventually*.

Now, given these levers, I can quickly run through combinations of settings to see how I'm covering the "decision space."

Keep it and staff it? Yeah, that's option 2.

Kill it and staff it? Yeah, that's option 3. Etc.

You can even sketch out a little plot of the space.

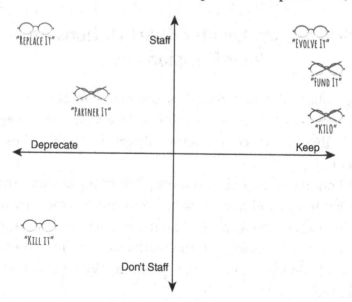

In this diagram, I used little glasses to represent those options on vision and those that aren't. Cute.

Using All the Parts of the Animal

When thinking through the levers that one can pull in creating options, I find that folks are often far too narrow. They only think about those levers that are:

- Their comfort zone and skill
- Fully owned by them

As someone who leads research and development, my managers often default to thinking the only lever they can pull is "write code and release software products." But when you have a problem with customers using your product, sometimes releasing more product is the worst thing you can do!

This is the old "Everything looks like a nail to a hammer" problem.

For my leaders, I'm always stressing that they have other tools beyond code at their disposal. What about partnering with marketing? Or sales? Or our customer onboarding team? If you want usage, you should really make sure we're talking about our product right, demoing it right, and setting it up properly for customers. A sales compensation plan is a product manager's best friend! If that's borked, making design and code changes is irrelevant.

You see, *great leaders* have this tendency to steal food from other people's plates. They use all the parts of the organizational animal. A great leader realizes there are levers that can be pulled that are outside of their skill set and authority. Call it collaboration if that helps! It's a blindness to organizational barriers and a humility with respect to leveraging capabilities and skills that aren't fully comfortable to the leader.

In my own Team Chat example, leveraging business development to use a partner for Team Chat leans into a function (biz dev) and a skill (partner negotiation) that I neither own nor fully understand (partners tend to hang up the phone on me).

Those kinds of cross-functional options should always be considered when trying to up your options-based decision-making game. Get someone else to do your homework if that's what's best!

Pull a "10th Man Rule"

In the film *World War Z*, starring a globe-trotting, zombie-fighting Brad Pitt, the 10th Man Rule is explained when Brad Pitt visits Jerusalem in the film.

For some reason, Israeli leaders had anticipated a global zombie outbreak and had built a wall around Jerusalem to keep all the zombies out. How had they done it? The answer was simple enough: in any situation, where all the leaders agreed on an option (in this case, they all agreed to do nothing because zombies are the stuff of fiction), one leader, "the 10th man," was required to assume *the opposite* and act accordingly. In this case, since everyone thought zombie rumors abroad were nonsense, one leader by necessity had to play devil's advocate (zombies are coming!) and act accordingly, in this case by building a wall around Jerusalem. Didn't matter much in the movie, because the zombies were pretty good at climbing walls, and everyone died, but the approach is still compelling!

In the case of a leadership problem, you should always take a little time to play devil's advocate with yourself on important problems or find a trusted partner (this can be a mentor, colleague, boss, direct report, spouse, kid, dog, or ferret) to play devil's advocate. You probably know someone whose way of connecting with you is always by disagreeing; put that oppositional defiant disorder to good use!

When I look at the options generated so far, there are some clear gaps. The chart is pretty helpful in visualizing the gaps as well as the options themselves. Specifically, I've got lots of options that lean into staffing the problem either for the purpose of killing or for keeping the product. But as for not staffing, well, I've got only one option there (if you're not going to staff the product, kill it!).

The 10th man would need to take on the gaps here: what would it mean to keep Team Chat but not staff it?

Well, in the extreme, this would be a disaster. Without a marginal amount of possibly fractional staff, if the product experienced stability issues, there'd be no one to fix them, and customers would be pissed. Pure neglect in this case is not good leadership (as much as I wish it were).

But as I thought longer, I realized that an option in this particular quadrant of "levers" was *offshoring*.

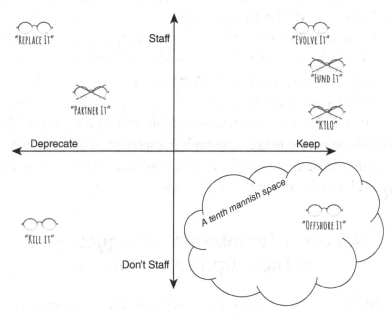

Option 7: Staff Team Chat offshore: While not completely staff-neutral, Team Chat's downsides actually lend itself to an offshoring option. Team Chat isn't integrated well with the rest of the product. It's siloed and off-strategy. If it could remain functional with marginal progress to meet customer needs, that would be good enough. And its marginal revenue would support a less expensive team of four offshore engineers and a leader at a 50 percent discount over U.S.-based staff.

Simply asking the question, "Is there really no way to keep this thing but not staff it?" led to an additional option!

Checking In on Our Exercise

Earlier in this chapter, you wrote down a problem you're trying to make a decision on in the worksheet on www.wiley.com/go/leadershipwise. I'd like you now to jot down all the options you can come up with for this problem.

If you just want to do the bare minimum and consult yourself in order to keep up the pace on reading this book, cool. But I'd encourage you to practice sourcing an option from each ring of the options-generating diagram. I think you'll find the exercise liberating, because everyone is capable of bringing their whole lives (your passions are a metaphor machine, your network is a sounding board, etc.) to bear here without needing to reshape themselves into someone they're not.

Wisdom Literature Would Suggest None of These Options Is "Wrong"

I'd like to return to this topic of wisdom literature that we discussed in the introduction of this book. Are any of these options clearly wrong at first glance? Not really! Now, they may be wrong given my context, i.e., my budget, my staff, the goals of the company and R&D, etc. But are any of them universally or principally wrong? I think not.

And that's where business books get a bit dangerous.

If I read a book about "focus," it's going to push for the options that eliminate distractions. The "Kill It" option for me will look mighty attractive (although killing a product is certainly a temporary distraction).

If I read a book about "customer centricity," it's going to push for options that provide value to the customer, and well, Team Chat does do that regardless of how off-vision it is. In that case, perhaps keeping the feature whether that's by keeping the lights on, fully staffing it, or offshoring it becomes the more attractive way to go.

Like I noted at the beginning of the chapter in that diagram with the radiating circles: business literature is good for *creating options* (what's an option that helps us focus as a company? What's an option that helps us keep the customer at the center?) more than it is for *filtering options*, i.e., making the decision.

At the stage of generating options, it's best to keep an open mind. Don't let your experience, the books you've read, the way your company does things, the attitude of your CEO, etc., narrow your thinking *yet*. Plenty of time for that later. For now, the best results come from pressing against these boundaries. In the words of *Proverbs*, let's consider both "answering a fool" and "not answering a fool." Or as Taco Bell famously put it, let's "think outside the bun."

Isn't This Overkill? "Paralysis by Analysis"

When I speak to people about generating options for important decisions as a leader, I often get folks who pooh-pooh the whole idea.

"We don't need leaders who can't trust themselves."

"If I generated options like this for every important decision I had to make, I'd never see my kids."

"This is paralysis by analysis. It's too slow. Your competition will eat your lunch while you're busy navel-gazing!"

I'd like to make three points with respect to this criticism.

Over-confidently Incorrect

First, the world is going to want you to think that the best leaders are those who have always had the best ideas deep down in themselves straight from the womb and have a preternatural confidence as to which way to go.

Do not confuse stubbornness with courage.

Do not confuse overconfidence with preternatural correctness.

There are circumstances in which a leader, based on practice, past experience, and education, knows easily which way to go; however, to believe that that ease will be the case in all or even most decisions *that matter* is the hallmark of a self-diluted and lazy leader who's playing a pop-culture version of greatness.

This Needn't Take Long

Second, the options-generating exercise we did in this chapter needn't take long and can be tailored to the importance of the decision. People like to create a strawman of options-based decision-making wherein the leader spends a month gathering all the possibilities, all the data, etc., meanwhile the world passes by until the opportunity to make the decision is gone.

Sometimes gathering options for an *important* decision does take a month or more! You may need to pull data or run an A/B test to validate options. But what I've detailed in this chapter needn't take much time at all! Talking to some colleagues? All in a day's work. Perhaps reaching out to some folks in your network? That's a text message or (yuck) a LinkedIn message.

Consulting your own brain? I do my best self-consultation in the shower sometime between the shampoo and the body wash.

Now, yes, asking yourself which decision levers you have available to pull and how your options fall into a possible space of decisions does *require intentionality*. But if a good leader is one who makes good decisions, then I think we can all agree that applying some intentionality to the most important part of the job isn't exactly asking much. It's literally the job description.

Analysis Paralysis Is All About Objectives, Not Options

As we close out the chapter, I want to address this idea of "analysis paralysis," which is the idea that a leader can become so enamored with all the possible solutions to a problem that they can't bring themselves to choose an option and move forward.

Only a sucker would seek to avoid such situations by never really generating a portfolio of solutions to a problem to begin with. That'd be like preferring a grocery store that stocks only plain Cheerios because it streamlines your grocery shopping decisions.

Now, analysis paralysis is real! I've seen plenty of leaders survey their possible options in making a decision only to sputter out and throw their hands up as to which way to go. But the reason for that hasn't to do with the options, and instead, it has everything to do with **their objective**.

And that's what we'll dig into in the Chapter 4! So, let's pack up the problem and its options you wrote on (**www.wiley.com/go/leadershipwise**) and let's move on to objectives.

4

What's Your Objective?

Some time ago I had a check-in with one of my product managers who could never be faulted for having too much creative energy. We were kicking off the year, and they were introspecting on the team they had and where they might take the team and product in the coming year. The product manager began to rattle off possible road-map items one after the other. Each possibility was compelling, and I was pumped. I wanted the team to build all the ideas!

The product manager then asked me, "Which idea do you think we should do? Any I'm missing?"

I knew better than to fall for the ol' escalating product road-map trap.

"All these options sound great to me for one reason or another," I said, "but it's not my job to pick between them. That's your job. It's my job to ensure that you pick the right objective that allows you to clearly pick between them!"

I felt like Galadriel rejecting Frodo's offer of Sauron's ring in *Lord of the Rings*. I'd passed this test and could remain chief product officer.

You see, generating and discussing options is always *the fun part*, but deciding between them correctly, well, that's the rub, isn't it? That's where clear leaders often leave the indecisive leaders behind. Here's a quick reference:

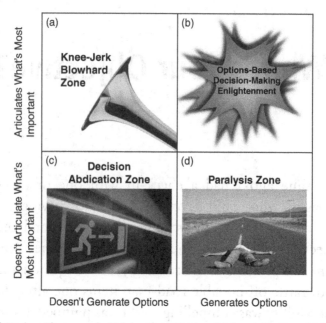

Source: (a) Davizro Photography/Adobe Stock Photos, (b) Seguir/Pixabay, (c) Семен Саливанчук/Adobe Stock Photos, (d) Jane Allan/Adobe Stock Photos

To choose between a bunch of options, like the road-map items my product manager was proposing, the leader must have a **clear objective**. Pros and cons have no worth without a priority that lets us know which are most important and which can be relatively ignored.

My product manager's job wasn't to create options and then escalate them to me to prioritize them. I'm always more than happy to use my gut to prioritize things for people, but remember, my gut is built primarily on Taco Bell and Haribo. The only thing it prioritizes effectively, as discussed extensively in Chapter 1, is shitting my pants. So best to rely on a stout objective rather than my caprices.

A Problem Isn't a Priority

If I told you I was going to drop you blindfolded into the wilderness and you had to get to safety, which would you choose: four gallons of water or a can of bear spray?

It's kind of hard to answer!

What if I pulled your blindfold off and this was the wilderness in question?

Source: byrdyak/Adobe Stock Photos

Welp, you could throw the water at the bear, but somehow I think the bear spray would be more effective. I'd also need a new pair of underwear.

Now what if I pulled your blindfold off and this was the wilderness in question?

Source: Tuxyso / Wikimedia Commons / CC BY-SA 3.0

I think the decision of what to choose to make it safely out of the wilderness just got a bit easier!

Often when we articulate problems we're trying to solve as leaders, we'll articulate a problem vaguely.

"What do I do about Bob? He's a B at best."

"What should we sell next?"

"How should sales and onboarding work together to set new customers up for success?"

There's nothing wrong with this to start. A simple, "What about Bob?" articulation of a problem gets the juices flowing, is enough to spark good conversations, and can fill a box full of possible options. That's what we saw in my Team Chat example in Chapter 3; "What do we do with Team Chat?" was enough to consult the team, my colleagues, my network, books, and more.

But such a coarse articulation of a problem is often not enough to choose between the options you end up generating.

"Make it safely out of the wilderness" just isn't enough. "Make it safely out of a forest full of Kodiak bears" or "Make it safely out of the desert as far as the eye can see" provides a bit more meat for choosing between options.

At the end of Chapter 3, I claimed that it's not having too many options that cripples leaders and causes analysis paralysis. No. Instead, it's not having a clearly defined problem statement, i.e., an objective that sifts your options easily based on *what's most important*.

In the case of my product manager I mentioned earlier, they knew what product they owned, and they knew they were vaguely supposed to "make it better" and "sell more of it," and based on the ideas they pitched, just "do cool shit with it."

But that's not enough, and their asking, "Which way do we go?" showed that they hadn't done their homework to ask themselves, "What's the most important objective for the team?"

It's not "get out of the wilderness." It's "get out of the wilderness *without dying of thirst*." We have to get tight if we're going to choose between options.

Two Words to Know and Love: Minimize and Maximize

So you want to solve a problem. How do you know when you've sufficiently defined your objective enough to sort through your options?

Have you worded your problem as *one thing* that you can objectively *minimize or maximize*?

Bob sucks, and you're wondering, "What should I do about Bob?" But what are you minimizing or maximizing here? What's most important to optimize for?

Perhaps it's *minimizing business disruption*? That would make it hard to remove Bob. We're going to have to make him better through lots of training, feedback, and coaching. Or we could "hot-swap" him for someone already up to speed. The option then might be to start interviewing while he's still in seat (you could have him unknowingly train his replacement if continuity is most important), which will make his firing abrupt, but the transition smoother for the business.

Perhaps it's *maximizing the effectiveness of the person doing the job* that Bob is currently employed to do. That would make axing Bob far more attractive than hoping to coach a B- up to a B+.

In Chapter 3, the problem I articulated was more or less, "I need to do something about this legacy, off-vision product called Team Chat." Well, that was enough to generate options, but is it enough to choose well between the options I'd articulated? Not really!

Why do I need to do something about Team Chat exactly? **What am I trying to minimize or maximize?**

In my case, the mission of Podium is to become the customer communication platform for local business, and Team Chat is a distraction. Every time we sell it, every time an engineer works on it, every time a customer uses it, we drift a little bit further off-mission.

What particularly bothers me is that our R&D department isn't huge right now. We're a few hundred folks, and that's counting us product managers who don't do anything all day but make Gantt charts about timelines. We have about 200 engineers, so it's the engineering time spent on Team Chat that bothers me the most.

Therefore, I might rephrase my problem as the following objective:

How do I minimize the engineering time spent on Team Chat?

The moment I write down this objective I start to struggle. Wait, is that what's most important? The product is off-strategy! Shouldn't the objective be to make it on-strategy at all costs?

As I think about that, the answer is no. I'd love for it to be on-vision, but when I think top-down about our platform as a whole, I'd rather engineers be spending their time building other on-vision platform capabilities. An on-vision version of Team Chat would be amazing, but it's not even in the top 10 products our vision demands we deliver over the next three years.

As I think through my options from Chapter 3, another question arises: am I minimizing the expenditure of resources in the short term or in the long term?

In this particular case, the answer is long term. This isn't about the next three to six months; I'm tired of having Team Chat hang over my head year after year. I'm in my third year at Podium now, and it's been a distraction each year. So, I reword my vague problem as a tighter objective:

How do I minimize the R&D resources working on Team Chat *in total over the long term*?

This objective frees up the maximum amount of staff to work on higher priority things over the long haul.

So now let's return to my options from Chapter 3.

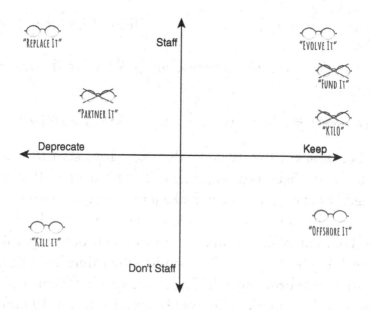

First things first then: the little glasses icon in my chart indicating whether an option is on- or off-vision, while interesting, isn't the priority! We're focused on reducing staff over the long term.

According to my objective then, "Kill It" wins the day. Sure, there'll be a flurry of short-term activity to kill the feature, but after it's gone, Team Chat will no longer bog anyone down. But even as I utter these words, I hear the voice of my CEO in my ear, "But what about the users who are already on it? What about that revenue?"

Is It Possible to Love Two Objectives at the Same Time?

Sometimes it can be very hard (if not impossible) to eliminate a seemingly just as important second objective. I contend, however, that the best leaders are objective monogamists; a "priority polycule" gets real messy real fast.

In my case, I care about freeing up R&D resources to work on the product vision, while my CEO, who's sympathetic to me, wants to know what happens to the revenue already tied to Team Chat.

There are a couple of things I could do in this moment that would be fail states:

- **Do both priorities at the same time:** Ever wanted an OREO and a ham sandwich, so you opened the OREO and slid a round slice of Canadian bacon on top of the cream filling? I sure hope you haven't! When faced with multiple competing priorities, the bad leader is the one who just says, "Uh, we'll try to do both," which usually means doing neither very well or subconsciously picking one over the other without fully admitting it. Like Ron Swanson said, don't half-ass two things; whole-ass one thing!

- **Completely reject one priority offhandedly due to pressure:** In this case, I could just jettison my priority of keeping engineers working on important things to keep the CEO happy. That's job security, right? Such an approach abdicates my leadership responsibility as the decision-maker here; if my CEO and I disagree on priorities, we need to have a conversation where we negotiate them.

Here's an AI-generated "OREO ham sandwich" to serve as a visual reminder:

Turning "priorities" plural (which is a logical contradiction embedded in a single word. . .the word *priorities* shouldn't by rights exist) into a single priority, then becomes one of the defining skills of a good leader.

This is yet another place where the business books of the world will fail to help you further. Your priority is *highly contextual.*

Do you "answer a fool" on Facebook who's posting about storming the U.S. Capitol on Jan. 6? Whew, buddy! That's a contextual call. What's your goal?

To choose between priorities and locate the **one true priority**, it's helpful to categorize the typical trade-offs (contradictory goals) in business that often create multiple priorities. Here's a nonexhaustive common list that you'll recognize as having overlap with the contradictions we walked through in Chapter 2:

- **Short-term vs. long-term goals:** In the short term, I might be trying to hit a quarterly booking target, but in the long term I might be trying to deliver a transformation product. Which is more important? Depends! This is the Team Chat trade-off that my CEO and I bump up against in the earlier example.

- **Growth vs. efficiency:** Prior to 2022, most of the companies I knew were in growth mode, and they were happy to burn cash to make it happen. Then interest rates went up, the markets crashed, and investors got skittish. All of a sudden efficiency became king. At many companies these two goals are always duking it out for supremacy.

- **Current vs. future customers:** Similar to long term versus short term, many priority decisions center around conflicts between keeping current customers happy and trying to attack a future, strategic customer base. This often comes up as companies seek to go up/down market, expand to new verticals and geographies, or expand product line offerings.

- **Speed versus quality/reliability:** Sometimes you want the best, and you want it fast. You often can't have both (unless dining at Taco Bell, of course).

By acknowledging these common trade-offs inherent in your priorities, you can evaluate which priority best aligns with any other company objectives, and more importantly, you can "uplevel" debates about priorities. I call this **priority decomposition**.

Generalizing the trade-offs inherent in your specific problem allows you to create a better shared vocabulary with others you might debate options with. Including yourself!

In the Team Chat case, this decomposition of the Team Chat problem into higher-level concerns can help create a language for my CEO and I to debate staffing engineers to more important work versus maintaining Team Chat–related revenue. In this case, we're talking about short-term goals and keeping current customers happy (preserve Team Chat revenue) versus long-term goals and serving future customers (staff engineers to things other than Team Chat).

By upleveling the conversation, we can at least check which of our priorities are in line with the highest-level priorities of the business. In this particular case, my CEO pointed out that the highest priority of the business for the year was working on SMB SaaS retention, usage, and churn. We'd all agreed at our previous offsite that that was the goal. We'd told the company at the beginning of the year in the company kickoff that was the goal. It was hard to disagree; by this logic then, preserving the revenue (and the associated happiness) of users on Team Chat became *the* priority. We agreed that Team Chat needn't print any new revenue. Its usage wasn't correlated with retention better than any of our more on-vision products. So, we were in retention, not expansion, mode only.

Ugh, I hate it when my CEO is right, and I'm wrong. OK. . .new priority: maximize the retained revenue coming from Team Chat.

Turn Priorities Into Constraints

But what do I do about my desire to staff as few engineers on Team Chat (maximize as many engineers staffed to on-vision work) over time? If that's not the priority, what is?

First, let's not make an OREO ham sandwich out of it! So often leaders will keep a secret priority in their back pocket and try to achieve it without anyone knowing. This is failure.

My best advice is to turn "secondary priorities" into constraints. It's not a perfect solution, but it's a little bit of a hack to help you filter out options.

In this case, I'll take my priority of "minimize the number of engineers" and turn it into a constraint. We've got about 200 engineers, so I'm going to allow 1 percent of the engineering staff (that's two engineers) to work on Team Chat. Looking through my product teams, if I put any more than two engineers on the legacy product, I'd have problems staffing the priorities that really matter.

Now I can reword my problem ("What do we do about Team Chat?") as the following objective and constraint:

Maximize the amount of revenue retained from Team Chat customers subject to keeping the engineer count staffed to the feature at or fewer than two engineers.

If I then return to my options from earlier, I can evaluate this objective. First, let's apply the "two engineer" rule to the options. In the following chart, I put a Comic Sans "2" next to the options that work. "Fund It," "Evolve It," and "Replace It" all take larger teams, so they're out; I'm unwilling to invest the people.

Out of those options that demand two or fewer engineers, which option maximizes the amount of revenue retained from Team Chat? Killing it is certainly not the way to go! Partnering with another company to frame something in is an option, but that may overturn the apple cart on existing revenue. "Keep the Lights On" is super attractive since it will keep the feature running for existing users; it's the option that's most squarely oriented toward revenue retention and nothing more. That said, the staffing solution for KTLO (engineers are staffed elsewhere, but they flex over to fix bugs as needed) will likely lead to more downtime than we'd like. Therefore, offshoring comes out as the best bet here. In fact, at offshore rates, I can probably staff four engineers to the product, which would be enough to not only keep the feature running but perhaps even iterate on it.

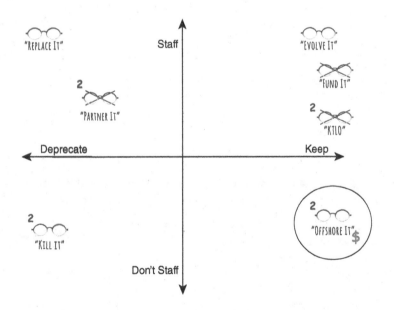

So there we have it! We've gathered options, we've refined our problem to include a real objective (we broke out the word *maximize*), we wrestled through competing objectives, and we located an option that might work best.

I want you now to return to the worksheet (**www.wiley.com/ go/leadershipwise**). Can you do the same? I want you to take your problem statement from earlier, and I want you to recast it as somewhere that can better filter your options. Can you specify a single priority? Can you employ the word *maximize* or *minimize*? Write down any competing priorities you might have, and think about how to let them go or to perhaps make them constraints.

Now look back at your options. Use your recast objective to sift your options better.

State clear reasons (be decisive!) for why an option subject to your objective and constraints sinks to the bottom or rises to the top! Cross out options or annotate them with your reasons.

And if you're ready, make a decision!

A Brief Interlude

want to pause here in the book. At this point, we've covered the basics of what you need to better structure a decision-making process for important decisions. To reiterate: simply making better decisions is **the number-one way** to be a better leader.

Given where we're at, let's just do a quick recap on what I've argued so far. It's actually pretty easy to sum up, so if you're looking for a way to speed read the book, maybe just read these few pages here.

Here's the recap:

- Business decisions are highly contextual. Surveying many categories of typical business decisions, it's apparent that common solutions to problems have *equally viable opposite approaches.*

- The best way to solve highly contextual problems *is not* to reduce them to something more general and apply the same basic solution repeatedly. This is a shame because:
  - As pattern matchers, we really like doing this.
  - As followers of idealized business personalities and stories, we really like doing this.
  - Business books tend to encourage this behavior.

- The best way to solve highly contextual problems is to *collect options* and select the best option according to what's most important, i.e., a *primary objective.*
  - Wisdom literature as a genre would back me up on this even if the landscape of modern business literature wouldn't necessarily.
  - There are lots of places we can go to collect options for solving problems both inside and outside the business and your industry. It's important to *cultivate a variety of options-gathering outlets* both close to and far from the locus of the problem.
  - Anything can be metaphorical inspiration for generative options exercises if we view it that way. Don't be ashamed to spend time watching *The Last of Us.* It's leadership homework.
  - When it comes time to sort your options for the best decision, make sure you spend time *defining what matters most to you.* This is where you avoid the dreaded "paralysis by analysis." Use those words *minimize* and *maximize.* Ruthlessly eliminate secondary priorities. Transform them into constraints rather than objectives if that helps.

And that's the book so far! You know. . .maybe I could have just led with that and saved us some reading, but I don't think so. There's a difference between showing someone a running automobile and taking them through how it all fits together and why. I'm glad we took our time to break things down, and ideally some of the tips and guidance I've provided at length have helped.

There's Plenty of Book Left!

Gosh, sounds like we're done, right? Not quite! I believe that any decision-maker could take what we've covered so far and use it to improve their performance for their organization. That said, there's still a lot to say about how one executes the process I've detailed *as effectively as possible*. You're not Spock, and neither are your co-workers. You're not operating in some super-rationale operational vacuum (emotions and company culture make sure of that). It's good to know how to check your work. Furthermore, a great decision is one that *considers execution and possible failure*. We need to do what we can to improve your chances of this process working well and yielding you **not just the best decision but ultimately the best business outcome**!

Let's keep going then. The back half of this book is going to get weirdly emotional even. It's going to be great.

5

Check Yourself Before You Wreck Yourself

In Chapter 4, we ended right at the point where we had what's required to sort options and make a decision.

In this chapter, I'd like to discuss *covering your ass*. How do you minimize the likelihood of failure for your decision? Pull more data!

How do you minimize the consequences of making a wrong decision? Iterate, learn, and take "two-way doors" (we'll define that shortly).

And how do you use your colleagues to check all your homework? That's the "premortem."

You can call it "second guessing yourself," but if you've got more data, you've got more input from your colleagues, and you're going with options that have less inherent risk, then second guessing is just good business. "Measure twice, cut once," right? (I know, I know.)

With each decision you make, how intensely you use the tools and approaches in this book can be modulated. If you're making a super important decision, please take your time and use more of the tools I'll present in this chapter. Less important decision? What we've done through Chapter 4 is more than enough.

Going Deeper with Data

Whenever making an important decision, one pass over the options that can be exceptionally helpful is "getting more data."

"No shit, Sherlock," is probably what you're thinking right now. Anyone who has the time and capacity to pull data that helps inform an important decision before making it would naturally do so.

Two thoughts then: First, sweet! Glad we're on the same page. Second, you'd be surprised how many leaders I encounter who consider pulling additional data to evaluate options to be a bad idea. They might say generally that it's a good idea (especially for *other leaders* to employ), but then in practice with any specific decision, they'll skip the step anyway.

Leaders tend to overestimate both the likelihood that they're right and the difficulty required to pull data needed to evaluate options a little more closely in equal measure.

There's a correlation between those who go for jobs that demand lots of decision-making (i.e., leadership roles) and being the type of person who just likes to make decisions, data be damned! That's why you find so many DISC Ds, Enneagram 3s and 8s, and Myers Briggs ETs in leadership roles. These folks jam bricks on the decision-making gas pedal, because that's their personality's comfort zone.

If that's you, then once again I'm asking you to practice a little self-understanding here. Know this about yourself and endeavor to more often pump the breaks, especially on large decisions, to gather more data. The question, however, is which data? Hell, what is data?

Is an Anecdote Data?

There's a scene in *Gilmore Girls* where the town nerd, a guy named Kirk, decides to do a Gallup poll to see who's going to win the election to become mayor of Stars Hollow, the fictional town in which the show is set.

Now, here's how Kirk executes that poll:

"The Gallup Poll uses a sample of 1,005 voters to represent the 280 million people of the United States. Using that logic, the correct sampling size of Stars Hollow would be .002. Rounding up that means one person needed to be polled. So I picked me." Kirk polled himself, and that was that!

It's absurd, but isn't that what leaders so often do? They poll one person and call it a Gallup poll.

A leader's favorite type of data is the lone anecdote. They talk to the one customer. They listen to the one sales call or read the one support ticket. They see the one stat (usually a stat from a *Harvard Business Review* article rather than from their own company data).

And while, yes, a single datapoint is still data (well, datum to be grammatically correct), it's, honestly, not.

Single anecdotes are most often used by leaders to confirm the thing they already want to do. And you as a leader, should try to avoid this style of head-up-your-own-butt, anecdotally of course, decision-making. If the anecdote is true, it'll hold up when talking to five customers or more. If the anecdote is true, your data in your databases is unlikely to contradict it. So for important decisions, take a beat, pop that favorite anecdotal evidence of yours back in its trophy case, and pull something more substantive.

Quantitative vs. Qualitative. . .Who Wants Pretty Good Pizza?

When talking about data that might better inform your decision-making, that data could look a whole bunch of ways. The word *data* often connotes "spreadsheet," and while I love a good pivot table as much as the next guy, that's not necessarily what I'm talking about. If my decision affects employees, then talking to some employees about the effects of the decision and getting their reactions can count as data. Sentiment can be data! So remember then that sometimes the data that fits the bill is qualitative, and sometimes it's quantitative. Both are acceptable, and both have their advantages and their drawbacks.

When thinking through the trade-offs between qual and quant, I like to think about it the way Michael Scott on *The Office* thinks about the difference between Alfredo's Pizza Cafe and Pizza by Alfredo. Michael asks, "What is better, a medium amount of good pizza, or all you can eat of pretty good pizza?"

A medium amount of good pizza? That's qualitative data, although it's usually just a small amount of good pizza.

All you can eat of pretty good pizza? Well, that's quant data.

More precisely, here are your data options:

- **Quantitative data** gives a precise answer (all you can eat) to an imprecise question (pretty good pizza).
- **Qualitative data** gives an imprecise answer (a small amount) to a precise question (good pizza).

Let's take my Team Chat example. One of the top areas of concern for me in making a decision about Team Chat is preserving revenue. So some revenue data then would be important to pull.

What if I asked an analyst to pull "How much revenue is Podium earning from Team Chat?" Could they answer that for me?

Podium sells *packages of products*, not individual products. So, the analyst could pull the total revenue of packages that *contain Team Chat*, or, better yet, the analyst would pull the total revenue from packages that contain Team Chat, where the user is actually *using Team Chat*.

That's a precise answer to a question, but it's not the answer to how much revenue Podium is earning from Team Chat. I might have users who would ask for a refund or discount if I removed Team Chat from their package even though they're not even using it. I might have users who'd stay and shrug and just use Slack or Microsoft Teams or even WhatsApp if I took Team Chat away from them. It's hard to answer my actual question precisely from quantitative data, because the quant data we have reflects our packaging structure rather than our line of products individually. So, the analyst can pull *a precise answer to an imprecise question*.

On the other hand, qualitative data often provides *an imprecise answer to the right question*. Going back to my Team Chat example, I could interview some customers who have Team Chat in their packages and find out exactly what they'd do if I took away the product. I couldn't do an interview with each customer, though. So, I'd have to make do with 10 to 20 interviews, which, while imprecise, would allow me to understand the percent who might actually cancel over such a change.

Oftentimes the best answer is the "chocolate-covered pretzel of analysis," i.e., a little salty and a little sweet, which is to say a *combination of both quant and qual*. Interview some folks who don't use Team Chat and find out how much they'd care if I took it away and didn't give them a discount. Interview some folks who do use it; what am I going to have to give them on average to keep them? Apply my interview findings to the quantitative data I have on both groups to get a sum total of the revenue effects if

I encased Team Chat in concrete and dropped it to the bottom of the Great Salt Lake today.

Priorities and Constraints Come First

When it comes to pulling additional data to evaluate your options, priorities and constraints come first. To rank your options according to your (singular!) priority, you need to have good data. If your priority is earning revenue, what data do you have that can support which option makes you the most revenue? The same would apply for any priority from employee retention to legal compliance to minimizing costs.

After that, consider your constraints. If you've got a budget constraint to your options, you'll need to get data on how each option hits the budget. Feel free to put a finger in the wind on the obvious things and pull more precise data when the options you're weighing get neck and neck. And if your data is in the "projections and estimates" camp (i.e., not so much data as it is a manipulation of past data to predict the future), then it's always helpful to get at least another set of eyes to double-check that math. As a product person, I have a lovely tendency to over-forecast demand and under-forecast bugs, so I sanity check such things with a colleague.

You Know What They Say About Assumptions

A simple exercise for figuring out what data you need to pull is simply to ask yourself, "What assumptions am I making without data?" Later in the chapter we'll discuss the practice of executing a "premortem." The "what assumptions" question is a great one to ask during premortem.

Any assumption you're making in sorting your options that's backed by gut feel, by "best practice" at other companies, by something you read, etc., might be precisely the area where pulling a little more data might be beneficial.

As always, calibrate the effort you put into this based on the importance of the decision. Running a SQL query isn't terribly hard, but transforming and moving data from other systems to build a database to query in the first place might be a challenge. Talking to five customers isn't terribly hard, but fielding a well-written survey to a few thousand customers might be a challenge. Calibrate accordingly.

Default to Learning Fast and Iterating

Let me ask you a totally reasonable question about a very realistic hypothetical situation.

Let's say that I blindfold you and Usain Bolt, and I plop you both in the center of Sanford Stadium in Athens, Georgia, home of the National Championship Georgia Bulldogs. Go Dawgs.

Now I place a million dollars somewhere on the sidelines of the football field, but you and Usain are both blindfolded, so you're not exactly sure where that loot is.

Remember, Usain is fast, as in the fastest human ever to walk (or run) the planet. And you, well, if you're reading a book on business leadership, odds are your strength isn't your speedy legs. But only one of you gets to have the million bucks, and that's going to be whoever finds it first. No peeking!

I offer you two ways to find the million dollars. Whichever method you pick, Usain has to go with the other method.

Method 1: We put a Bluetooth headset on your head. You get to choose a buddy, and they get to sit in the stands of Sanford Stadium with a pair of binoculars, and they're gonna call you and talk you through how to get to the million bucks. *But* they can say only two words, "hotter" and "colder," and they get to say those words only **whenever your feet touch a sideline**.

Method 2: This is the same basic idea except your buddy can say "hotter" or "colder" to you **every second**.

Which one are you going to go with?

I'd pick Method 2 and force Usain to go with Method 1 for the very obvious reason that my partner would get to talk to me sooner and more often. Why? Because it would take me more than a second to reach a sideline even if I wasn't running blind. I can't beat Usain in a footrace, but if he's moving the wrong way, even for a few seconds, maybe I could win.

Getting feedback on decisions quickly so we can change course and try something better is a big deal! I'd rather adjust my course more often in the correct direction than run like a bat out of hell too long in the wrong direction.

And that's not just when I'm blindfold racing an Olympian in a football stadium; that's a mathematical reality.

Not All Who Wander Are Lost

Back in grad school, I studied mathematics applied to decision-making. Fascinating, I know. That's why I ended up working on everything from pricing berths for Royal Caribbean to building models for Coca-Cola that told them what barrels of orange juice pulp to thaw in China.

Well, one of the things I learned about in grad school was the difference between "deterministic" algorithms for solving decision-making problems and "probabilistic search-based" algorithms for solving decision-making problems.

Deterministic algorithms followed a recipe, and that recipe, when followed long enough, would eventually arrive at *the answer*. We all know a few deterministic algorithms by heart. Long division and multiplication are good examples. You follow the long multiplication *algorithm* and eventually you get an answer, right?

In contrast, probabilistic search-based algorithms don't have a set recipe for cooking up an answer to a problem. Instead, they search the space of possible solutions, learning along the way what makes a good or bad answer ("hotter!" versus "colder!"), until they settle on a great answer.

What I learned in school is that for simple stuff, the recipes always performed the best. Follow the recipe, and you'll get your answer quickly. But as decision-making problems got increasingly complex and possible trade-offs got super weird (I might say "nonlinear"), suddenly search-based approaches became competitive, and then eventually they became the fastest way to go and sometimes *the only way to go*. In a complex space, these algorithms would search the space of options quickly, trying out thousands of possible answers in mere seconds, making their way toward the correct solution. They were like Dr. Strange in *Infinity War* searching millions of realities to figure out how to beat the villain. It was awesome.

So how does this apply to business?

Humans are the most complex things in the universe I would argue (this might be a religious argument more than a scientific one). No one can even describe to me why certain people like kombucha, which is a fairly basic phenomenon. That's how complex we are: some people like kombucha even though it clearly tastes awful.

Now what's a business? It's a bunch of humans (super complex things) running around bumping into each other to sell goods and services to a bunch of other humans running around bumping into each other.

That's complexity squared!

So, business problems look *a lot* like these crazy nonlinear decision-making problems I was studying in grad school. This means we can do better in business by **trying things fast, searching the space of decisions, iterating quickly, failing, learning, and moving on.**

This then is an argument for choosing options in making a decision where:

- You can learn how the decision is doing at multiple points along the way.
- You can pivot if things don't work out, i.e., take an "off-ramp" when you learn how it's going.

In other words, you want an option that can tell you whether you're headed toward the million bucks in the corner of Sanford Stadium *fast* so you can adjust course!

Solving a problem using an option that takes a long time to indicate whether it's successful isn't ideal (how do you know the path you're on leads to a right answer?), especially when contrasted with an option that can give feedback sooner. And that's especially true if that feedback allows you to adjust the option you've taken!

In software, we take this approach all the time by favoring releasing "minimum viable products," i.e., "shitty first drafts" instead of fully baked products. Online software is easy to adjust once you learn what customers like and don't like about it. Are they buying? Are they canceling? Adjust!

But favoring options that give fast feedback and provide off-ramps for adjusting as you go isn't limited to software.

You can prototype and market test hardware.

You can create a company that's able to evaluate performance well and **fire fast**.

You can embed milestones in long projects with specific goals that a project has to hit to unlock funding.

Create and favor options that allow for learning as you go and changing the option (or changing your mind entirely) if possible.

Tying this approach to the previous section on pulling data, if you're making a decision that doesn't provide a lot of good data (e.g., let's say you're making half-baked projections about future demand where you've gotta *believe* some assumptions about the market), then you're in a scenario where a search-based approach is definitely needed.

And when you're in a search-based situation, i.e., a situation where you're making lots of assumptions, data is scarce, and confidence is low, then the types of options that will suit you best are "two-way doors." Let's talk through what those are.

One-way vs. Two-Way Doors. . .or Are They Streets? Two-Way Things

Every day on the way to work in Atlanta, I used to pass by a mural painted in large letters that said "Never give up." That mural always bothered me for the same reasons that caused me to write this book.

Really? Never? Never give up? The leaders I've worked with who never gave up were some of the worst, most blind, leaders I've ever seen.

They'd quote Churchill plenty, "Never give in, never give in, never, never, never, never—in nothing, great or small, large or petty."

It's this sentiment that caused your buddy to stay trying to make it as a singer-songwriter for half a decade too long. We've made the "indefatigable leader" a contextless ideal when, in fact, like all things in business and in life, "It depends." Hell, even George Washington is famous for knowing when to retreat. Like I said at the beginning of this book, wisdom is choosing between "holding 'em" and "folding 'em."

You see, people never finish that Churchill quote, "Never give in except to convictions of honor and good sense." **When it makes good sense to quit, it's a bad leader that doesn't.**

So let's talk about quitting, and let's talk about how we *embed quitting into our decision-making process.*

Way back in 1997, which is a shockingly longer ago than I thought it was, Jeff Bezos, the world's most quotable bald entrepreneur, said the following:

> *"Some decisions are consequential and irreversible or nearly irreversible—one-way doors—and these decisions must be made methodically, carefully, slowly, with great deliberation and consultation. If you walk through and don't like what you see on the other side, you can't get back to where you were before.*
>
> *But most decisions aren't like that—they are changeable, reversible—they're two-way doors. If you've made a suboptimal Type 2 decision, you don't have to live with the consequences for that long. You can reopen the door and go back through."*

I'd encourage everyone to take Bezos' one-way versus two-way door advice to heart when making a decision, but I think we need to break apart his use of the word *decision* into this book's framework of "problem" and "options."

Sometimes you have a "one-way door" problem. This means that any solution to it, i.e., every option, is a one-way door.

I used to work in the "expiring inventory" pricing world, meaning hotel rooms, cruise ship berths, airline seats. This inventory all expired; i.e., the moment the ship set sail, the moment the night turned over, the moment the plane took off you couldn't sell that thing anymore.

My job was to create mathematical models to set prices that would maximize revenue for these items. The problem itself was a one-way door problem. You had a limited time to sell inventory, and then that inventory was gone forever, literally set sail into the sunset. You had to pick a price at each moment, and when you listed the berth or seat or room, then that was the price at that time, but you had to pick something! Sure, you could change the price later up until the actual date of departure or stay, but you wouldn't get yesterday back if you had listed it too high and demand went to a competitor. And if you listed too low, well, if someone bought it at that price, fair was fair, and you missed out on revenue that they were willing to hand over.

That's a one-way door at the problem level. And if you encounter such a problem, then slow down, get more data, consult more folks, get your priorities straight, and make a good decision, because you're living with it! In my case, I got all the historical demand and pricing data the companies had to set prices the best I could.

That said, as leaders, so often the one-way door isn't at the problem level but *at the option level*; i.e., there are some one-way options and some two-way options.

In that case, not all options are created equal! If you go with a one-way option, you're done solving this problem. And sometimes the best option is a one-way, and you just have to go for it. YOLO.

But on balance, if you have the opportunity to choose between a one-way door and a two-way door, the two-way door option has a leg up, because if the option fails, you can go back through that door and select a different option.

Let's take a look back at my Team Chat decision. Now, I don't know how doors get labeled as one-way and two-way, so I mixed my metaphors and labeled my options using one- and two-way street signs.

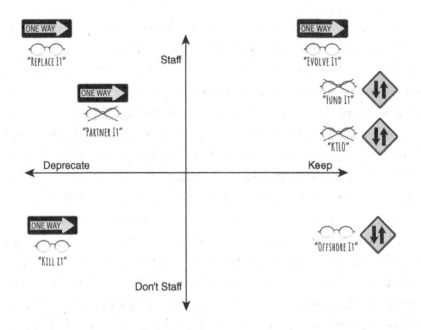

Any option that deprecates (kills) Team Chat is clearly a one-way door. Likewise, evolving Team Chat into something new (my Brussels sprout option from Chapter 3) is likewise going to effectively kill the old Team Chat. So it too is a one-way door.

Meanwhile, simply funding the product, funding it with an offshore team, or keeping the lights on with borrowed help from other teams, well, those options don't do anything irreversible to the product itself nor do they prevent me from changing my mind and, say, killing the product later.

In the case of using an offshore team to care and feed for Team Chat, this makes for an interesting point. Sure, Podium doesn't have a ton of experience with fully offshore development, but if we get it wrong, we can backpedal.

Now, a couple words of caution here.

First, two-way doors **are not free**. You still lose time (that's opportunity cost), and you can expend all sorts of resources going through a two-way door and back again. In my case with going offshore, sure, I can change my mind, but there are legal, financial, and organizational costs for going through that door and for going back through it if I don't like what's on the other side.

Second, don't dismiss all one-way doors out of hand. Sometimes the best decision just so happens to be the one that requires changing the company permanently, and if that's the way it has to be, so be it. But it's best to engage in that decision with your eyes wide open. In the end then, the one-way versus two-way door angle is just that, an angle to take in evaluating your options, perhaps best used as a tie-breaker for decisions that are neck and neck.

Do a Premortem

So far we've covered pulling more data to better assess your options and, in complex and ambiguous decisions, favoring options that allow you to learn, fail, and iterate faster. You're covering your ass as they say. You're minimizing both the likelihood of being wrong *and* the consequences of being wrong. In this chapter, I want to cover a final way of minimizing *both* the likelihood that you're making a poor decision and the consequences of being wrong: the **premortem**. It's easy, it's social, and it'll up your decision-making game.

Both at Mailchimp and at Podium, we employed penetration testers to ensure our applications were secure against intruders. Penetration testing is conceptually pretty simple: you pay an outside firm to try to hack you. Sounds like awesome work if you can get it! Imagine that: "getting paid to break into people's places so that other people can't break into their places." That's actually a quote from my favorite movie of all time, the 1990 film *Sneakers*, which is about penetration testers.

At the beginning of the film, Robert Redford and his team of "sneakers" are paid to sneak into Centurian Bank and present to bank executives how exactly they did it. So Robert Redford fakes a fire in the bank in the middle of the night, which unlocks the fire escape door, through which they enter the bank and use the bank's computer system to fraudulently deposit cash into an account. The next day they then walk through the front door and legitimately withdraw their fake deposit. Clever! If you do one thing based on reading this book, I hope it's watching *Sneakers*. I digress.

What Centurian Bank paid for (as does Podium), while terribly enjoyable, is actually good, healthy leadership. Penetration testing is a clear example of *assuming that you're wrong so that you can be right*. Sometimes we talk about "putting something through its paces." This is an example of putting security through its paces. Kicking the tires. Taking it for a test-drive.

Everyone knows the term *postmortem*. A postmortem is an examination of a death *after the fact*, and it's a staple of every murder drama you've ever watched. We do postmortems in business all the time, and they're a healthy way to learn and iterate. Why did a product release not go as planned? Doing a blameless postmortem can be a helpful way to share learnings and do better next time.

But what do you do *before you make a decision?* Well, that's a premortem! A premortem asks the question "why might this thing die?" *ahead of time*.

The premortem is a common tool used in business (I certainly didn't come up with it), and it's a great way to kick the tires on a decision once you've zeroed in on your favored option.

The activity is simple enough. You've selected a decision, i.e., an option you're going to go with out of your space of possible options. Now you ask the simple question:

Down the road, when it's all said and done, why did this decision fail?

This whole book I've been encouraging exercises in "meta-cognition," which is basically "thinking about your thinking." This is a great little metacognitive practice in that you're pushing against all the supposedly great thinking that led you to this decision.

Now, if you want to set a table for one and do the premortem by yourself, you absolutely can do that, and I often do, especially for smaller decisions. I also have a habit of talking to myself in the shower and when I drive, so this feels pretty natural to me. If I'm gonna mutter, might as well be productive in my muttering. That said, the best premortems involve pulling in trusted partners.

Indeed, many of the folks you'll want to invite to a premortem discussion are the same folks you sourced options from at your company as we discussed in Chapter 3. If you trusted them to offer up an option, why not trust them to shoot holes in the one you've selected?

Now decisions fail for a myriad of reasons in business. Customers don't like things, competitors make moves, operations internally break down, you don't have the expertise you need, funding isn't made available, hiring is difficult, etc. I find that for the most important decisions then, a premortem is best executed with a trusted *cross-functional* group of peers that can represent the perspectives of each part of the business that participates in the decision.

If your decisions might fail based on something that happens in sales, customer support, marketing, finance, etc., then a representative from that group would make a great participant at the premortem.

OK, so we've got our list of attendees for such a meeting. Remember, you're walking into the meeting with them, *having already selected the option* you're going to go with. If you haven't tentatively made a decision, then the meeting will become a "decision by committee" group thinking exercise, and you don't want to weigh options live in real time with a bunch of people if it can be avoided. Committees are best for criticism and editing, not for decisiveness.

The purpose of a premortem is to gather criticism to refine the details of your decision *to increase the likelihood of success*. The purpose is not to reject the option you've selected and send you back to the drawing board, although that does happen.

Here then is my advice for how to run a premortem (don't feel like you've got to make this formal; I don't):

1. **Set the scene.** Explain to everyone the decision you've made. Be as transparent as possible in the process you've taken, the inputs and options you've considered, and the path you've decided to take. But be brief. Explain to everyone that you're engaging in a premortem. Why might the option you've selected fail?

2. **Collect feedback.** Timebox the exercise. If someone isn't participating or hasn't given feedback from their function's perspective, solicit that criticism directly (e.g., "Hey, Beth. Based on this decision, sales will have to change how they sell our product. How's that going to go?").

3. **Rank feedback.** After you've collected folks' concerns, do a quick sort either in the meeting as a group or afterward based on: **likelihood** that the concern will materialize during execution and **impact** to the decision. Now when thinking about impact, keep in mind your problem's **objective** (Chapter 4). Feedback can specify all sorts of impacts for your decision, but we care most about the impact to our objective. If I'm making a decision about Podium's Team Chat primarily to *preserve SaaS revenue*, then naturally I care about feedback concerning how this objective might or might not be achieved.

A high-likelihood, low-impact concern might be worth just absorbing, while a high-likelihood, high-impact concern can't be ignored. If you're a former consultant, this is a good time to pull out the old "two by two" chart! In this case, you'd simply plot the concerns on a grid where likelihood is along the x-axis and impact is on the y-axis; stuff in the top right would be the freakiest.

4. **Reassess.** Consider adjusting your decision. Oftentimes a premortem won't change a decision in any fundamental way. Rather, the premortem provides considerations for *how to best execute* the decision. This could mean changing timing or pace, changing budget or resourcing, creating better communications, etc., while still staying the course at a high level.

In the case of my Team Chat example, here's how a premortem would work. It's not complicated.

Podium already has a weekly executive meeting on the books to discuss what's going on in product-land. Leaders from disciplines across the business attend, and they'd be affected by offshoring Team Chat, so I would just use that weekly meeting as my venue for a premortem.

"After thinking through a bunch of options, including lots of input from y'all, I think our best course of action for Team Chat is to offshore the product," at which point I'd take the folks in the room through my logic in brief, and then I'd ask, "OK, so if we go this route, where does it fail?"

I'd gather the feedback, making sure to call on folks who remain silent to reflect on impacts to their area of the business specifically. After gathering the feedback on my decision, I'd likely chart probabilities and impacts *later*. I could do it in the room, but that's an expensive meeting. I referred to the ol' consulting "two by two" earlier. Here's what it might look like for me. Since Podium hasn't ever had a fully offshore development team to date (we do slot some Brazilian engineers into our US-based dev efforts on a smaller scale), many of the concerns are around the operations and security of such a team.

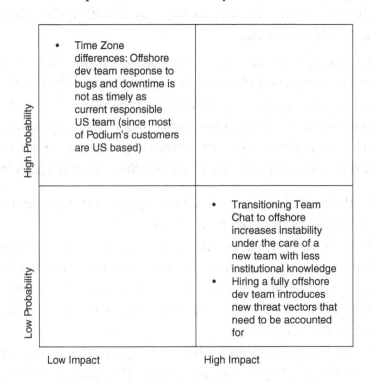

	Low Impact	High Impact
High Probability	• Time Zone differences: Offshore dev team response to bugs and downtime is not as timely as current responsible US team (since most of Podium's customers are US based)	
Low Probability		• Transitioning Team Chat to offshore increases instability under the care of a new team with less institutional knowledge • Hiring a fully offshore dev team introduces new threat vectors that need to be accounted for

Based on this feedback, I would adjust my decision. There's nothing here that makes me want to go back to the drawing board and reevaluate all my options. Rather, this feedback gets into execution. How do we handle offshore dev team hiring, training, and knowledge transfer? How do we handle security?

All right, so that's the premortem. Stick it in your toolbox and use it to fine-tune your big decisions before putting them into practice.

Blazing Through Covering Your Ass

Now you've got a few tools for buttoning up the decision-making process detailed through Chapter 4. You can pull some qual and quant data; bias toward learning and iterating, especially by using two-way doors; and can kick the tires on your decision in a premortem.

None of these things needs to take *all that long*.

Even for a large decision, I can carefully phrase the objective, source options, prioritize them, consider two-way doors in prioritization, and hold a premortem all within an 8-hour day. I've done it! You can too.

Pulling data, I will admit, can take time depending on your needs. For some decisions, pulling data can mean running a test that takes months. For other decisions it might be a simple database query that takes 30 minutes of an analyst's time. But you can pull as little or as much as needed to suit the importance of your problem and the timescale on which your decision must be made.

The point here is that while this can *feel like a lot*, it's not. While you may argue, "This is all too heavy and burdensome and takes too long," you would be better served by practicing this approach and getting speedy at it than by reverting to the ol' "shoot from the hip" decision-making.

When I first learned to "clean and jerk" a barbell (bring it from the floor to above my head), everything looked disjointed and unnatural. I did everything step-by-step in a rigid manner. Bring barbell from floor to thighs, then from thighs to collarbone, then collarbone overhead. As I practiced, the movement became faster and far more fluid.

That's what I'm talking about here. Once you get used to these things, you can execute them naturally, even conversationally. Give it a shot, and if it doesn't work send me an email at john.4man+complaints@gmail.com.

6

Making the Most of Execution

When I was a kid, there was a cartoon on TV called "Pinky and the Brain." The Brain and Pinky are both genetically enhanced mice who live together in a lab. The Brain is a genius who is determined to "take over the world!" He comes up with *perfect* plans for doing this, everything from controlling tornados to turning himself into Mousezilla. But the Brain's plans always fail *in execution*, usually because his sidekick Pinky is a bumbling idiot. This piece of execution, that The Brain doesn't have much to work with except a fool of a sidekick, is usually not considered in The Brain's plans. It's a clear picture of the "best laid plans of mice and mice" not necessarily resulting in success.

Have you ever heard the phrase "execution over strategy?" The idea is simple: those who *do well* outperform those who *plan well*. A mediocre strategy with excellent execution can beat a great strategy with subpar execution. This idea is about hustle: "putting in the work" as they say.

I don't think this sentiment is wrong! I will say that it's a far better adage in industries where strategies can be easily evolved and "two way doors" are plentiful. After all, if you can't change course often, then as Yogi Berra said, "If you don't know where you are going, you'll end up someplace else." It's almost like in the case of strategy versus execution (honestly, a false dichotomy), "It depends!" Someone should write a book about that.

To protect the sales of *this book*, please let me first point out that decision-making and strategy are not the same thing. You can make strategic decisions, yes. But you also make important tactical decisions as a leader. Either can be difficult. Either can be extremely important.

Some decision-making is as simple as, "To hit our goals, the sales team needs to make X sales a day. To make that happen, they need to make Y calls a day. We're going to hold them accountable to Y." The holding accountable is execution, but is the decision to hold the sales team accountable really strategy? Nah. It's an *execution decision.*

Indeed, what often sets apart good execution from bad are the additional decisions that are made during execution. In this chapter, I want to provide some advice not only for making good decisions but for producing good outcomes through executing those decisions well. This is not a book on execution, so I won't be exhaustive in what makes for good execution of a decision. Instead, I'm going to focus on those decision-centric elements of execution.

Make Your Decisions "Fully Loaded"

Ben Franklin once said, "By failing to prepare, you are preparing to fail." Good execution requires good preparation, and that preparation begins not after you've selected an option to execute but *as part of selecting which option to execute.*

When I talk about the best leaders being those who make good decisions, so often the good decisions made by those leaders are what I call "fully loaded decisions." Like a baked potato that comes with chili, bacon, cheese, chives, and sour cream already on it, a fully loaded decision is better than one that ignores execution in its articulation of the path forward (that'd be a boring, plain potato).

By this I mean that the decision-making process (what I outlined in Chapters 1–4) includes execution considerations in sourcing and ranking options. It's entirely possible that an execution concern (staff, budget, timeline) can be the *primary objective* of a decision-making process. More often we see these execution concerns embed themselves in the decision-making process in a couple ways:

- **Including only *viable options*:** There's no need to evaluate and consider options that are completely outside the realm of operational viability. Yes, an option exists for Team Chat that's in the vein of "peel out of primary app, staff to make better than Slack, take Team Chat to market as its own incredible business chat app." But is it operationally viable? In terms of the staff and budget required, absolutely not. There's nothing wrong with rejecting such options immediately. We need to be realistic and honest here, of course, but do be careful not to be too much of a change curmudgeon.

If your tendency is to think small and go for safe bets, then I encourage you to actually back off a bit here. If your tendency is to get into trouble by biting off more than the organization can chew, then lean in here.

- **Embedding operational concerns as constraints into the process:** You can rank options according to your objective but *subject to operational constraints* such as available staff, available funds, timeline, institutional knowledge and capability, ability to measure progress and success, and more! In fact, this is just a better-structured version of the previous bullet where you're dismissing options out of hand because of their egregious violation of implicit constraints.

The important point to remember here is that **decision and execution are not two distinct phases** of a process where you make a call devoid of execution concerns and then hand it over the wall to someone else to execute. Execution bleeds up into the decision-making process when done well.

Furthermore, in Chapter 5, we discussed digging deeper into decisions at length, and the approaches presented there make for great avenues for considering execution and planning ahead. In particular, the premortem is an excellent tool for incorporating execution preparation early in the decision-making process.

When executing a pre-mortem of a decision, some of the top attendees of such a conversation should be those who will play a substantial role in executing that decision. If I'm making a decision on redesigning Podium, I'd better have some designers and front-end engineers in the premortem room! If I'm going to reprice and repackage the product, I'd better have finance, sales, and marketing in the premortem room! That's how you source the operational complexity of an option that can cause you to refine the decision or change it altogether.

"Use All the Parts of the Animal"

In my experience, the best fully loaded decisions pay careful attention to the *who*. And the best leaders carry their decisions forward into reality in a way that not only considers the steps of execution but also **all parties needed to fully succeed**. In fact, the best leaders will, in the course of creating and choosing between options, manipulate who's involved in execution in order to pull in as much effort from different folks as possible to succeed.

In Chapter 5, we discussed the importance of inviting those who serve an important role in execution of a decision to the premortem for that decision. That's one specific example of a generally important behavior: a good leader leverages all functions of the business to ensure the success of a decision during execution.

Riffing on *Field of Dreams*, I'm fond of telling folks in R&D at Podium, "If you build it, they *won't* come." What do I mean?

There are two types of product leaders at Podium.

To start, we have the classic "canned product manager" who's read enough blog posts and books to understand and execute the most important mechanics of the job. They gather customer feedback, they develop product development roadmaps, they work with design to help visualize what we're building, and they work with engineering to bring that visualized road map to life. So often, these product managers will release products that all their data says the customer wants. And their well-tested designs are great! It's engineered well, too! But the product flops like a wet noodle.

What's up? Well, their product was a tree that fell in a forest where no one was around to hear the sound of its falling.

By contrast, we have the "all parts of the animal product manager." They know in their bones that "If you build it, they *won't* come." Specifically, a product, even well-executed, is worthless if there's been no attention paid to pricing and packaging it, marketing it, selling it, and onboarding it. This second type of product manager spends a fair bit of time making sure marketing knows what's coming, how to talk about, who to talk to, when, etc. They spend time with finance, marketing, and sales getting the pricing and packaging just right to make things attractive for customers and easy for our customer-facing teams. They spend time thinking through how a new customer will onboard and use the product effectively so as to not churn out. They use every part of the business (that's the "animal" in this metaphor) to ensure that their product is successful; they realize that no amount of beautiful design and performant code can compensate for a lack of customer awareness. So, they engage all the teams in the business to be successful.

A crap product in the hands of an "all the parts of the animal product manager" will often *outperform* a good product in the hands of a standard product manager.

Now, this book is about making good decisions not necessarily execution, so let's bring it back around. When considering options in the context of their own execution (i.e., "fully loaded"), *right then is the time to begin identifying the parts of the animal that can be leveraged in execution for success.*

For example, perhaps you've got two options to choose from in making a decision. One of those options leverages only engineering to solve a problem. The other leverages sales and marketing, design, engineering, and finance. You might skew toward the engineering problem then because all those other teams are busy, or you might skew toward the animal with more parts because each of those teams provides value that increases the chances of success and impact of the decision. Sure it's more "herding cats," as they say, but with each added function of the business, you *get more firepower*.

So, take an accounting of all the teams and functions that can be leveraged to make a decision succeed *up front*, and then exploit those teams to win when entering into execution.

Establish Success and Failure Criteria Up Front

Churchill once said, "However beautiful the strategy, you should occasionally look at the results."

One of the downsides of my philosophy on decision-making is that if in business there aren't necessarily clear right and wrong answers, then we have to accept that in this often-gray and complex world we're going to get things wrong. Sometimes, "wrong" can look like a dumpster fire, while other times, "wrong" can look like a smaller fire burning in a barrel. How do we know if we judged well or judged poorly? Well, we need to define that up front!

There's a scene in *Indiana and the Last Crusade* where a Nazi sympathizer named Walter guesses which cup Jesus drank from at the Last Supper. If he guesses right and drinks from the Holy Grail, he gets eternal life. Not a bad payoff for simply taking a drink. However, as the film puts it, Walter "chooses poorly," and he rapidly ages, his skin shrivels, and he turns into a skeleton. Boom, he's one dead Nazi.

Now, Walter makes a number of errors in choosing the cup of Christ. If he'd read this book, he would've done a far better job in sourcing and evaluating options for which cup to choose from. But one of the main errors Walter makes is he never asks the simple question, "What does failure look like?"

Had he asked, someone (the "grail knight" if you've watched the film) might have told him that failure looked like turning into a human raisin! Prune? Craisin? Shriveled fruit of some kind. Let's not be Walter.

Similar to defining what failure looks like, we also need to know what success looks like ahead of time. The ability to describe succinctly what it means for our decision to be successful is a prerequisite to ranking options because it's linked to articulating your primary objective. If my objective is maximizing revenue, then success might be defined as achieving a certain amount of revenue in a time frame (and failure might likewise be associated with a lower range or a later time frame).

Defining success and failure explicitly in terms of data and measurements is then what allows us to not only rank options, pull the right quantitative and qualitative data to add color, execute better pre-mortems, etc., it's also what allows us to continuously evaluate the option selected *as we execute* in order to understand how things are going.

Why is this important?

In Chapter 5, I recommended choosing options that are two-way doors, i.e., options with easier **off-ramps** that allow us to undo them as a business and go back to the drawing board. But you generally go back through a two-way door only once you've decided, "Nope, that didn't work!" And you want to make that call as soon as possible. That means creating measurements of success and failure that can be evaluated along the way.

I'll give an example from Podium. A little over a year ago, Podium had a mobile app for iOS and Android written in a programming language called React Native. Now, the name is a bit of a misnomer because what it actually meant was that we didn't have an app that was actually written natively to leverage the best that iOS and Android had to offer in their operating systems. Our app was buggy. It logged customers out all the time. Notifications didn't work well. On Android, we had a 2.6 star rating, which, frankly, was embarrassing.

The mobile development team came to me and the CTO and made a proposal. They wanted to rewrite the React Native app as two separate truly native apps: one for iOS and one for Android. They'd be written using all the tools that Google and Apple provide for making great apps. This wouldn't be cheap! We'd need two well-staffed teams, one for each operating system. But the result would supposedly be more reliable mobile experiences for our customers, higher app store reviews, and ultimately lower customer churn. Well, I was a bit skeptical, honestly. I always say the three horsemen of the product apocalypse are "replatform, rearchitect, and refactor," and here was a team wanting to do a full rewrite!

This is going to take forever, I thought.

In making the call as to whether to allow the teams to attack mobile app development in this way, we evaluated other options, we defined our priorities, and ultimately we gave them a green light.

But not without defining what success and failure looked like! The decision to rewrite the app was a two-way door because we wouldn't sunset the old React Native version until we had something to replace it with (the old Indiana Jones swapping an idol for a bag of sand trick, although in our case, we'd be swapping a garbage app for a shiny new one). Success, we said, looked like replacing the old app with a rewrite that was more stable and functional *in a single year's time*. That new app would need to include just about all the functionality of the existing app because we already had a ton of revenue tied to the mobile app's features. Failure looked like pushing a boulder uphill forever. We deemed failure to be any rewrite that took longer than a year or that didn't provide most of the functionality in the existing app. Why? Because that would leave customers using not only the old crappy app, but they'd be using an old crappy app that no one was caring for all that much because they were busy writing a new one!

Having defined what success and failure looked like and acknowledging that with this two-way door we could basically get off the ride at any time, we established checkpoints for the team. They had to have certain pieces of the rewrite done by certain dates or else we were taking the two-way door, i.e., calling the project dead and reverting to the old app.

Every 6 weeks we met with the team and checked in on those milestones. And every 6 weeks they knocked it out of the park. It was a very happy ending for all involved. But defining success and failure was important for the team and for leadership. It kept the team focused. It kept leadership from meddling overly much or from getting cold feet.

But what if your decision is a one-way door? The same thing applies! Because even one-way door decisions can be tweaked and evolved.

Maybe you've made a decision from which there's "no coming back" as a company. Defining success and failure criteria that can be evaluated along the way still allows you to change course in the details. If you're off schedule, for example, you may need to replace a manager, funnel in more budget, or tweak a design. The project still proceeds, but you know where you stand.

At Podium, one tool we use in this vein is that we define **"tripwires"** for ongoing efforts and operational decisions. When we set a goal, we also define a tripwire, which is a point where our performance is *too far from a goal*. For example, when we released our phones product, we not only set a sales goal for phones in the first half of the year, we also set a tripwire—if we sold fewer phones than the tripwire, we knew we needed to have a serious conversation with cross-department leaders about what was going on.

Tripwires are specific measurements of failure that *trigger* important conversations and additional information gathering in order to make adjustments to your course. But if you don't set them, then you don't know when you've tripped them!

Be Transparent, But Commit to the Bit!

OK, no more delaying! You're making a big decision, and you've done the following:

1. Defined the objective clearly.

2. Sourced a bunch of options from those close to and far from the problem. You've defined the whole decision space according to the levers you can pull and made sure to leave no corner of that space unoptioned.

3. Ranked the options according to your objective.

4. Adjusted and perhaps reranked your options after you've pulled more data and possibly run a premortem. You've considered which options allow you to iterate and learn and which are "two-way doors."

5. Considered execution in your options and especially when executing a premortem.

6. **Made your decision**, complete with success and failure criteria.

It's time to go! All right, sweet, well, in that case I've got two **behaviors** for you. They're simple. Anyone regardless of personality can do these two behaviors. I'm not asking you to become more charismatic, more salesy, more pensive, more stylish, or nerdier. No need to get a septum ring. No need to dye those gray hairs. These are easy behavioral changes, but nevertheless, they ensure your decision has the highest odds of succeeding. And these two behaviors go right back to our definition of leadership at the beginning of the book as someone who "makes decisions that *affect other people*."

Since our decisions have to be executed by others and since they affect others, the following two behaviors are essential from you as a leader:

- **Be as transparent as possible** about your decision-making process. Communicate the "why" clearly.
- **"Commit to the bit."** Regardless of the odds of failure, regardless of approaching off-ramps, regardless of the decision being a two-way door, be fully committed to success.

By being transparent and communicating the why, we get others bought in to see the decision through. By committing ourselves to the decision, we get ourselves on board as well as those who look to us to model good behavior. And teamwork makes the decision work.

Transparency Costs You Nothing

It concerns me when a leader isn't transparent about how they've arrived at a decision they've made. Is it because their reasoning isn't buttoned up, so they can't possibly share their work? They don't want to say, "This *felt right to me*." Is it because they think that somehow letting folks into their logic invites criticism or the need to litigate the decision?

Either way, it's not good.

If a leader is being capricious, that's a recipe for a bad call. If a leader is being cagey to assert authority, then their concept of authority is bound up in some pretty ugly culturally driven assumptions about preternaturally correct leaders spouting decisions like religious canon. Speaking of religious canon, I've seen religious leaders act this way about as much as any other type of leader. I wish pastors would read a book like this because they too often combine knee-jerk decision-making with a supposed rubber stamp from God; as a group, they're some of the most powerful, worst-trained decision-makers on the planet. And I say that as someone who sits under pastors every Sunday. I digress.

I've found that by taking folks through the logic behind a decision, discussing the primary objective and the options and reasons for selecting the path you've selected, you actually can earn the confidence and buy-in of those you lead. Let them see "how the sausage is made," because if you're following the processes detailed in this book, that's some high-quality sausage! **Leaders are not magicians; their power lies not in their mystique but in the quality of their decisions**.

For example, I once had to make some changes to R&D spending that resulted in some folks in my department not getting what they had expected in terms of headcount, travel, and software spend. In fact, some of my most important employees had their job responsibilities significantly altered and made more difficult by how I re-allocated spending. I knew that communicating the changes I was making was going to be difficult for some folks. So how did I approach it?

I was transparent! I told them what I and the rest of the leadership team were trying to accomplish with the budget, i.e., what our primary objective was. I clued them into my constraints in making my budget allocation decisions. I ran down the list of options I'd considered, and I took them through who I'd consulted with in creating the options for deploying my budget. I acknowledged the positives *and the negatives* of the option I'd selected. And I told people why it was the best path to take.

Was the conversation easy? No! But I was able to show empathy and humanity to my team, and they in turn were able to empathize with the decision I needed to make. No longer were we in some sort of "management just doesn't get it" situation.

Transparency builds *trust*, and trust is one of the primary features that distinguishes a *team* from a group of folks merely working alongside each other.

Remember, this **transparency costs you nothing**. If you think it lessens some mystique you might carry around, most people probably find that mystique irritating anyway. You're human just like all of us. We're all just making the best decisions we can.

What's "My Part of Our Whole?"

So, transparency helps folks understand both the objective and rationale behind a decision, and it helps build trust, but there's a third benefit to transparency: defining roles early.

Transparency is a gift for execution because it creates a moment at the very beginning of a decision journey to help folks understand *their part* of the whole.

Teams at work, just as in sports, share unified goals even though each member of the team might play a different position. As a boy, I played soccer, and while I sucked at ball control, I *loved* to slide tackle people. My role on the team was slide tackling anyone who came close to the goal. It was a limited role, but I knew what I was supposed to do. Nevertheless, I shared a common goal with the rest of the team: to win by scoring while making sure the opponent did not.

When taking folks through a decision then, we create an opportunity to define roles very clearly. Here is what we're doing as a team, here is the goal, and here is *what I need you to do to help us achieve the goal.*

Never waste a decision as a moment for helping define folks' roles and how their work helps the company achieve success. Not only then will your transparency build trust, it can invigorate and motivate.

To summarize then, when making a decision, be transparent with those affected in order to:

- Unify the team around a goal
- Build trust
- Define each person's part of the whole

Commit to the Bit

In Chapter 5, we discussed how options that allow off-ramps for iteration or two-way doors should be valued more highly. In this chapter, we discussed how setting criteria for failure can help us know when to take just such an off-ramp.

These are healthy things to think through! We need to prepare for our decisions to fail, and the best leaders walk into decisions with eyes wide open both about the likelihood of failure and where the exit doors are in case of a fire.

That said, we must proceed *as if* the decision will succeed.

Whether you're pulling from psychology, from sports, or from religion, we don't have to look far to find a discussion of "manifesting" decisions, "faking it 'til we make it," envisioning success, or having courage (doing a thing despite our fears).

This commitment to a decision is essential when putting a decision into practice, especially a decision arrived at through the process I've detailed in this book!

Making decisions by searching the space of options and being clear about your priorities (so clear in fact that you can be transparent with others) removes any mystery surrounding a decision. You and your team, your company, etc., will walk into that decision with eyes wide open rather than blissfully unaware. But they do say "Ignorance is bliss!" How many of us have heard a successful entrepreneur say, "I wouldn't have attempted what I did had I known what I know now." Must be nice! But in this process, we've done our best to know as much up front as possible when making a decision. There's no going back to being ignorant.

Instead, we need to give a decision our all *in spite* of knowing the drawbacks and the exits. This is an exercise in cognitive dissonance that is required of you as a leader: to be both a realist and an optimist. At Podium the way we describe this leadership tension is with the phrase (borrowed from Patrick Collison of Stripe) "macro optimism, micro pessimism." We execute with the knowledge that we will ultimately succeed while keeping our eyes open for how things may go slightly off the rails from time to time.

This commitment to a decision is important for two reasons.

- As I mentioned at the beginning of the chapter, the best decisions in the world can fail in execution. And you as a leader undoubtedly have work to do in execution personally. Do your part to the best of your ability.

- Leadership decisions affect others and require others to execute. Folks at the company will *look to you as a model* and will mold their opinions and behaviors after your own. Your commitment or lack thereof will be seen and will be mimicked. Decisions paired with a lack of commitment are usually self-fulfilling failures.

There Is No Separation of Mind and Body

Whenever I go to the gym after having a great day at work, I notice that somehow *magically* I'm stronger. Whenever I go to the gym in a foul mood after a hard day at work, I notice that somehow *magically* I'm weaker.

My mind, my mental state, my confidence, and ultimately my ability to envision success are all tied to my physical ability to actually succeed. As integrated beings, our muscles' abilities are tied to our mind in strange ways that we can't separate as hard as we might try.

Decision-making (the mind) and execution (the body) are likewise intertwined.

Having an excellent ability to execute (we'll call that "huge muscles," which, alas, I personally do not have) but having poor abilities to choose well between options (we'll call that a "weak mind") will lead to failure. Similarly, all the best thinking in the world devoid of muscles will lead to getting crushed!

Instead, we need to acknowledge this integration in our decision-making. Create options that are fully loaded and consider each part of the animal, establish success and failure criteria for execution up front, be transparent in your decision, and commit!

CHAPTER 7

"Keeping It Real"

"Knowing yourself is the beginning of all wisdom."

—Aristotle

In previous chapters, I've alluded to "knee-jerk reactions" and your emotional, personality-driven tendency to go with the same types of options in your decision-making again and again. In this chapter, we're going to dive directly into that topic, which is going to feel very different from the preceding six chapters. This is going to be the weirdest, most uncomfortable part of this anti-business-book business book.

Previously we've talked about setting priorities, generating options for solving problems and sorting them, pulling more data, running premortems, etc. Very cerebral! Very dry. But we're *integrated beings* with reasoning that's always touched by emotion, so we have to understand that side of our decision-making better if we're going to have any hope of improving it overall.

Right at the top, I want to credit Bob Lewis, founder of Lewis Leadership and my executive coach while I was at Mailchimp, with helping me make sense of how emotions influence decision-making. Much of the content in this chapter originates with Bob.

Emotions Are Shortcuts

Conflict-averse people tend to, well, avoid conflict in the options they choose.

Conflict-seeking people tend to do the opposite. It's their personality. It's their emotional makeup.

Now, is this an entirely bad thing?

No!

Recently, I went back and listened to an episode of the radio show and podcast *Radiolab* called "Overcome by Emotion" (you can find it online at https://radiolab.org/episodes/91642-overcome-by-emotion). In the episode, the hosts talk about a man who had a brain tumor that cut his mind off from his emotions. Suddenly simple decisions, like choosing whether to use a black pen or a blue pen or choosing cereal in the grocery store, became insurmountable. How do you choose between two boring Bic pens if you can't say, "I just felt like it?"

Our emotional reactions are cooked-down stews of experience built up over time based on lived and observed causes (problems and resulting decisions) and effects (outcomes of those decisions) that lead us to make choices quickly and easily. Emotions are shortcuts for summing up our experience! That's not a bad thing. All emotions are neutral, neither good nor bad, and those feelings help nudge us in the direction of certain decisions quicker than our reason might otherwise.

I associate Wheaties with my childhood, with safety, with luxuriously free Saturdays. I'm roaming the cereal aisle hungry.

My emotions say, "Grab the Wheaties and be comforted." It's a shortcut in the decision-making process that can come in handy. After all, humans have to make thousands of decisions a day.

How in the world would you choose what to wear each day if you didn't have emotional responses to your closet? Ugh, I'm so tired of wearing that shirt. Time to try something new.

That said, business decisions as a leader can often be too important and too complex to relegate purely to the realm of feelings. It could be that you've got great instincts (which I'll define as the decisions we tend to choose quickly when guided by our subconscious mind and feelings) and those instincts got us promoted or hired into the jobs we're in. Our feelings might have a "good track record." That's awesome. But no one has ever walked the earth that's gotten it always right by following their gut. And if you're this far into the book, I suspect your gut has led you astray before too; otherwise, you've just read a bunch about making better decisions just to gloat.

This is why I talk in Chapter 3 about your emotional reaction to a problem being an excellent source for *generating that first option for solving a problem*, but not the best instrument for choosing between options when it comes to more important, complex decisions. Your emotional brain is an excellent resource! Use it—just not exclusively.

After you get that first emotional option for solving a problem, *you have to pause*, move to the level above your emotions where you "think about your thinking," and evaluate additional options. Now, I'll admit, sometimes getting beyond your emotions is *extremely difficult*, and I want to illustrate this using my own emotional hang-ups. Let me give a little autobiography. We're gonna get deep here, and if this isn't super comfortable for you (especially in a business book!), just hang with me; we'll pull back up and get practical I swear.

Diving a Little Deeper into My
Knee-Jerk Reactions

"Angry people are not always wise."

—Jane Austen, *Pride and Prejudice*

I was born into a home of two pretty smart Yankees. My dad, an English professor, grew up in the New England area, while my mother, an attorney, grew up in Pittsburgh. When I was young, we all moved to Lookout Mountain, Tennessee.

Lookout Mountain is a small town outside Chattanooga that is full of old money. The town's residents were mostly conservative and very southern. A lot of families on Lookout Mountain had been there for generations.

It was a terribly hard scene to break into as a boy who wasn't from 'round those parts. My parents voted the wrong way. My mother worked outside the home. I didn't have southern graces like putting "sirs" and "ma'ams" in my sentences at the right places. And time and again I was rejected socially by my peers. I dressed oddly, and I knew nothing of their social rituals whether that was swimming at the country club in summer or heading to the Smokies in the fall. They spoke of having a "legacy" at the local prep schools, and at the age of nine, most of my peers could tell me where they were destined for college.

I had no idea what SEC football was.

What's Hilton Head?

No, I don't know how to dove hunt.

I was a fish out of water, and wanted desperately to belong. I decided that the way to fit in and be accepted by my peers, was simply to be more competent than them. It would be hard for them to look down on me if I performed better than they did. I used to get so excited when my standardized test scores would arrive in the mail so I could see if I got in the "99th percentile" with a little asterisk next to it indicating that I'd gotten a perfect score. I figured that while I wasn't a prep school legacy kid, I could still beat out those kids on pure merit.

As I grew older, this focus on *merit* embedded itself deeper and deeper in my psyche. I attended the University of Georgia where I studied mathematics, and it was there, doing math problems that sometimes took me days to solve per problem, that I learned a helpful (and not so helpful) lesson:

> *If I just applied everything that I had in me, if I just sat and stared at a wall trying to crack a problem for hours and hours and days and days, I could crack it.*

I found that I had this superpower in college where, as I applied stress and pressure to myself, I felt my mind rise to the challenge as if the anxiety actually fueled some sort of clarity. I used that "dark side of the Force" to solve many a math problem. It worked! I called it "powering up" like Super Saiyan in *Dragon Ball Z*. I'm cringing as I write this.

My values of hard work, focus, and winning on merit began to concretize, and an emotional tendency in myself began to surface: *control.*

Learning that I could solve a math problem if I just applied myself wasn't a bad lesson. And the desire to control everything, to focus everything, to produce the outcome that merited the A grade wasn't terrible, mostly because it just impacted myself and my life.

Then something changed.

I went to grad school, I got a job, and I started managing people. I got married and had kids.

All of a sudden, both at work and at home, the outcomes I wanted to achieve *were dependent on other people.*

At home, things wouldn't go the way I wanted unless my kids did what I wanted them to do, whether that was being quiet in church, eating politely at a restaurant, or not spilling a Coke in the car.

At work, things wouldn't go the way I wanted unless my colleagues, my direct reports, and teams around me and under me did what I needed them to do.

What I'd learned as a kid up through college was that through my own hard work and intense focus I could create the results I wanted. I was an unstoppable force, but when I applied that unstoppable force to the immovable objects that were my children, I didn't get the same results that I got when I was just working math problems. I became stressed and frustrated. I became angry.

The same went for work. I wanted teams to produce certain outcomes that I had in my head, and I tried to force teams to do everything I wanted to a T. I began to micromanage folks; I'd get visibly frustrated when things weren't going well. When people didn't meet my high standards, I could be ruthless, often using sarcasm to belittle folks. I took the same approach to managing large teams that I had applied to my math homework in college: just funnel stress and pressure into a situation to focus myself (and, now, those around me) until I finally got the outcome I wanted.

To stay on top of all the micromanaging, I slept less and less, and I consumed coffee and energy drinks like water. I'd stay up late and work once everyone went to bed. The COO I worked with once commented that there was no time of day when they couldn't get an immediate response from me on Slack. And they were right. I prided myself on being on top of everything all the time. If the world was a meritocracy, and if I was going to prove to all the people who made me feel like an outsider that *I belonged*, then I had to succeed, and no one else could be trusted with that mission. Other people weren't capable; they were a disappointment.

What a way to live! You may be asking the question, "John, why did you so desperately want acceptance from a bunch of people you viewed as incompetent *anyway*?" Yeah, I'm not sure either. You ever make a bad decision and then make a worse one to fix the bad one? Like getting hung over drinking cheap wine and smoking cigars and then trying to fix it in the morning with a little "hair of the dog?" That's where I was.

It all came to head, though. Some years ago I was in a meeting about a product, and I was asked a question about a product decision that needed to be made. Under normal circumstances I'd have been able to just rattle off a bunch of context behind a decision, a couple paths we might take to move forward, and give a recommendation. But on this day, for whatever reason, I couldn't remember one of the options I had in mind. It was on the tip of my tongue, but it just wouldn't come to mind. I stuttered, and suddenly, an internal chemical dam broke. I felt a flutter of panic. Shortly thereafter I had my first full-out panic attack.

In fact, I had a panic attack so bad that I felt I couldn't breathe for two days before finally taking myself to the ER to see if I had a pulmonary embolism. After a battery of tests, a nurse handed me a sheet of paper titled "Symptoms of anxiety."

How embarrassing. I wasn't dying. I was just killing myself.

For the next week, I was drowning in panic. I'd sit in meetings struggling to pay attention while feeling like the cops were arresting me over and over and over again. My face was numb. I felt if I drank in front of people, the drink might just pour from my numb lips onto the table. My arms were numb. I had intense bouts of pareidolia, OCD symptoms, insomnia, and depression.

I believe that in my desire to control everything and everyone around me, I *broke myself* and was quite literally and painfully experiencing what might be called a "nervous breakdown" by some.

I had to change my life. I got into counseling. I started sleeping more and watching my caffeine. I stopped pushing through colds and working anyway. I put away the laptop after dinner.

What's the point of this long personal story?

You see, I had developed a "deeply held belief" (this is a term Bob Lewis developed), and that deeply held belief gave way to a set of emotional knee-jerk reactions and behaviors over the course of decades. My deeply held belief was:

> *"To be approved, respected, accepted, and, ultimately, loved (and to not be disapproved, disrespected, rejected, and abandoned), I need to demonstrate and prove without a doubt my superior competence in every performance situation."*

This deeply held belief not only justified but even compelled me to impose my "competence" (in quotes because I wasn't all that competent) by criticizing others and taking control. In my head that went something like this:

> *"Everyone is incompetent and not to be trusted with important work, so micromanage everything, do it all yourself, and fly at as low an altitude as you can. Make all decisions. Criticize everything. And apply fear liberally."*

So when faced with decisions my knee-jerk reaction was never to delegate, never to pull additional data, never to speak to teams on the ground or colleagues to source better options. No! Certainly not.

My knee-jerk reaction was generally to "power up" and seize control, fuel my brain with as much anxiety as I could muster, and pull the best decision I could come up with out of my own ass; it was the only ass that was to be trusted.

This, of course, demoralized teams and led to unhealthy processes and suboptimal decisions. Because I'm actually really bad at a lot of stuff. I shouldn't be trusted to design things, market things, conjure product road maps out of whole cloth, etc.

My emotional shortcut, my little "life hack," that helped me solve math homework in college had metastasized into something rather unhelpful in more complex business decisions.

So, how did I rein this in? With a lot of time and a lot of help! But we'll get to that, because that's what I ultimately want to discuss in this chapter. How do you change your knee-jerk reactions into knee-jerk *not-so-reactions*? And how do you slowly, over time, change those emotional and behavioral patterns in your life that get in the way of making the best decisions?

All Feelings Are Valid. Always Acting Out of Them Is Neither Authentic nor Beneficial

I made a promise at the beginning of this book that I was not going to write yet another leadership book where I attempt to convince you to fake a new personality to be more like some titan of industry. There will be no black turtlenecks in this book! And I intend to deliver on that promise.

But in this chapter, we're talking about getting beyond our knee-jerk tendencies when making decisions. How is that done in a way that's *not* wrapping yourself in some new personality? Well, I'm talking about *maturing*, and maturity is evolutionary and continuous; it's growing in those qualities that make us special and shedding those qualities that are unproductive for ourselves, our health, and those around us. By contrast, faking a new personality based on the advice of some business book is merely a recipe for exhaustion. As Marisa Franco puts it in her book *Platonic* while criticizing one of the most famous business books of all time, *How to Win Friends and Influence People*, "There's a psychological toll to faking. . .Suppressing who we are is labor." Shots fired!

We don't want to fake being some idealized leader; we want to mature our personality into one more suited for leadership! Now, so often folks criticize maturity indirectly, which is to say pausing and thinking about our thinking before reacting, as a *lack of authenticity*.

"But my feelings are valid."

"That's just *who I am*."

"I'm just being me."

"I'm just *keeping it real*."

"You hired me for what I bring to the table."

I believe these are all statements that pit a supposed *authenticity* against maturity.

There's a grain of truth in all these statements of protest. Feelings are real, neutral things; they are valid to the extent that they exist and convey often-subconscious information worth paying attention to. We don't want folks to be "fake" (be disingenuous, play politics), which at face value is the opposite of "keeping it real." We do hire folks for their strengths, which so often are tied to their instinctual reactions and decisions.

At the same time, it would be a mistake to stop at just "keeping it real," at just thinking "our feelings are valid."

My yellow lab's hunger is real and valid. That's what led him to eat an entire two sticks of butter, still wrapped in paper, off the counter. His actions that *stemmed from his feelings*, however, gave him the runs pretty bad. But we're not yellow Labradors. We're humans! What sets us apart from yellow Labs (and animals in general) is our ability to think about our feelings, think about our beliefs that propel our feelings, and engage in specific practices to best channel those feelings in a way that provides better outcomes.

I love the following quote from Marisa Franco's *Platonic* again, because she gets right at this: "Authenticity is a state of presence we access when we aren't hijacked by threat. It's who we are underneath our defense mechanisms."

Problems that arise in business, well, those are just threats. They're barriers to be overcome. And our defense mechanisms are our emotional responses and knee-jerk reactions; they're our go-to tactics for overcoming barriers. For me, that was "powering up" to attack problems. I'd encounter a barrier, like a project at work that was going too slowly or was drifting from the product vision, and I'd power up, criticize others, take control of the work, and dismiss any fallout I left in my wake.

But authenticity is not just acting out of those knee-jerk reactions. That's "keeping it real," but that's *not authentic*. Authenticity is understanding yourself enough to know what your knee-jerk reaction is, taking a beat to acknowledge your knee-jerk reaction (Franco uses the phrase "state of presence" in this vein), and then choosing the best path forward regardless of whether it's your knee-jerk preference or not. Because authenticity is about *acting from a place of self-understanding*, not from a place of direct emotion-to-action connection.

My dog was just keeping it real when he ate the butter, but he does not have the ability to act out of a level of metacognition and self-knowledge reserved only for humans.

So how do we make decisions more authentically?

A Process for Becoming Increasingly Authentic

I'm not a psychologist, but for this section, I'm going to borrow from basic behavior modification concepts that are employed broadly in techniques such as ABA therapy. Chiefly, I'm borrowing from Bob Lewis of Lewis Leadership whose content on emotional management was exceptionally helpful to me in my own career.

Let's start by diagramming our common decision-making tendency:

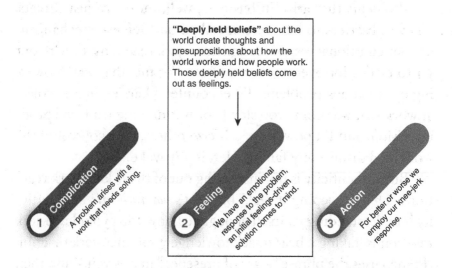

Bing bang boom. It's that simple. Where does everything go off the rails in the previous diagram? It's between your feelings and your actions! You feel a certain way. OK, that's fine. That's just a feeling. That's valid! But then you act out of it, and that's when things go from "my feelings are valid" to "shit just got real."

To implement the advice in Chapters 1–4, which is all about intentional, rational decision-making, we must *break the connection between steps 2 and 3 a bit*. But how? As Radiolab pointed out, "Just stop feeling" is not only impossible, it's also not helpful! We're humans, not Vulcans.

We might be inclined to *change our feelings*. If we don't feel a certain way in step 2, then we won't act a certain way in step 3, right? It is, in practice, extremely hard to change our feelings *directly*. George Costanza on *Seinfeld* famously tried to change his anxious feelings by repeating "serenity now" over and over, but the only result was him anxiously shouting "Serenity now!" He became more neurotic, not less.

Similarly, changing our deeply held beliefs, fueled by years of experience that lie behind our feelings, isn't done easily or directly either. So we're going to take an indirect approach.

What we want to aspire to is **inserting a pause** between "Feeling" and "Action" and break them apart since that's where the problem arises.

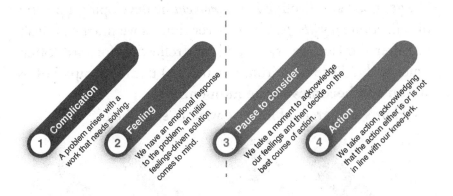

The important thing here is I'm not directly changing my feelings. I'm merely separating them from the actions I take so that I might choose better. Maybe that is indeed choosing as my feelings dictate, maybe not! But either way, I'm making that choice **consciously rather than subconsciously**.

"Pause to consider" in the previous diagram can be as short as a number of countable seconds or as long as days when it comes to making big decisions. Indeed, **Chapters 1–5 of this book all fit in the "pause to consider" step.** So, you can see why I'm so invested in creating this space for reflection. Without it, my book doesn't function.

Easier said than done though, right!? I mean. . .just today I reacted to my children out of frustration without pausing to reflect and consider the best options for how to respond to their behavior.

Being able to take this pause is one of the hallmarks of the best leaders I've ever encountered. So how do we get good at this? Maybe "good" is even too strong a word. How do we even get middling at this?!

Start with Post Facto Reflection

We get good at reflecting *in the moment* by developing a practice of reflection *after the fact*. Then over time as we practice reflecting after the fact, we try to pull that reflection forward (oftentimes with a little help from our friends) until it **jumps before action and becomes in the moment.**

Here's a diagram of how we want to start then:

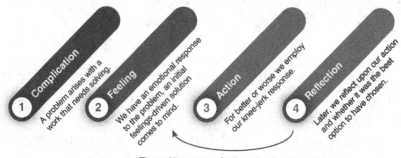

1 **Complication** A problem arises with a work that needs solving.

2 **Feeling** We have an emotional response to the problem, an initial feelings-driven solution comes to mind.

3 **Action** For better or worse we employ our knee-jerk response.

4 **Reflection** Later, we reflect upon our action and whether it was the best option to have chosen.

The goal is to move reflection to be *ahead of action*.

If you struggle with emotional responses, you'll want to develop some regular, habitual practice for reflection on your actions. This can look all kinds of ways. I'll give several examples I've seen work for people:

- **Counseling and executive coaching:** I've used counselors and executive coaches as sounding boards for talking through the ways in which I've reacted to problems and made knee-jerk decisions in the moment. For me, Bob Lewis was a godsend of after-the-fact reflection where I was able to say to Bob, "Whoops. . .I did it again. . .I made people believe I'm an asshole." We could then talk through how I felt during a knee-jerk reaction and the beliefs that propelled those reactions forward.

- **Leaning on a trusted partner:** It doesn't have to be a professional. This can be someone inside or outside work who you can talk to and discuss how the week has gone and where you acted in a knee-jerk fashion. This someone can help you identify patterns in the situations that cause this. I've seen folks use spouses, priests, best friends, online communities, and support groups.

- **Practicing some type of meditation:** Take up a practice of reflecting on your day (or yesterday if you're a morning person). In my religious tradition, we have a meditation called "The Daily Examen" that's an accounting for the highs and lows of the day that St. Ignatius created 500 years ago. I suspect in whatever tradition you follow, there exist practices for quiet reflection. Many of us have a capacity for honest self-reflection that can be just as effective as using a sounding board.

- **Journaling:** Similar to meditation, you're pausing to reflect and jot down how things are going.

As you reflect on the actions you've taken out of your emotions, you'll grow in awareness of your tendencies, so much so that you can begin to pause *in the moment* and reflect. Now, for certain decisions, the ones that really "push your buttons," this is going to take practice—sometimes you'll succeed, and sometimes you'll fail. This won't be a linear progression! For me, I failed so much that I needed to recruit some help at work.

This was the one tactic that Bob Lewis recommended for me, which I employed at work, that was quite helpful: I recruited a number of allies, people I trusted to have my best interest at heart and who worked with me frequently, to merely say the words, "John, you're doing it again," to me.

John, you're doing it again.

That's all they had to say. And when they said it, I knew exactly what they meant. John, you're reacting instead of consciously acting. You're seizing control needlessly.

Here are the basics of how that recruiting conversation went:

"Hey, so you know how sometimes I get frustrated in meetings and then I make bad decisions out of that frustration, like barking at people or being unnecessarily harsh or taking control of their work?"

"You mean like every Tuesday and Thursday and sometimes all the other days of the week?"

"Yeah, pretty much."

"I am well aware of your, uh, 'tendency.'"

"Whenever I'm doing it, can you just say, 'John, you're doing it again?,' and if we're in a big meeting, just text it to me if you can or give me a stern look with a furrowed brow or something."

"Yeah, no problem."

It's that straightforward. A conversation like this might be humbling for you. It might be a little embarrassing to admit you have a problem. But the best co-workers know that you're all on the same side, striving to create great outcomes for the business, and they'll know that by holding you accountable to improving your behavior, everyone benefits. The best co-workers will see this as a sign of strength, not weakness.

Positive Reinforcement Is the Feedback Loop That May in Fact *Change You*

While I said that I'm not *trying* to change your personality in this book, I'll admit that if you follow my advice, you might actually end up becoming a healthier version of your personality, which is to say more mature, i.e., a person who acts far less out of unhelpful deeply held beliefs that are so often either outright lies or at least bad generalizations of the complex world in which we live. We can become more open people, more "it depends" people (which is to say "wise"), rather than dictatorial people who always choose the same paths for better or worse.

How does this advice end up changing us? Well, our subconscious mind *loves a good reward*. B.F. Skinner and Pavlov's dog and all that. And as we incorporate pausing after our feelings to reflect on our options, and as we choose different options on occasion that our feelings might dictate, we **create a feedback loop to our beliefs and emotions**.

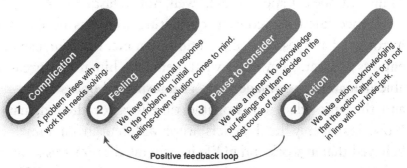

1 **Complication** — A problem arises with a work that needs solving.

2 **Feeling** — We have an emotional response to the problem, an initial feelings-driven solution comes to mind.

3 **Pause to consider** — We take a moment to acknowledge our feelings and then decide on the best course of action.

4 **Action** — We take action, acknowledging that the action either is or is not in line with our knee-jerk.

Positive feedback loop

As we make more intentional decisions, which have a tendency to work out better than knee-jerk decisions, our deeply held beliefs and associated emotions *can change*.

When I began to pause and consider decisions rather than always seizing control ("John, you're doing it again"), I found that there were moments when I was OK with extending more trust and more authority to others I worked with. Lo and behold, many of those folks *delivered*. There was a reward for my rational decision: good outcomes were created without me staying up until midnight "rage Slacking."

Those rewards fed back into my brain, and over time I noticed my beliefs about the world and my feelings that stemmed from those beliefs (my knee-jerk reactions) changing. I no longer believed everyone was incompetent. I was able to delegate better. And it didn't take away my ability to hold people accountable. But it certainly was more sustainable.

That's Cool. But It Doesn't Apply *to Me*

I find that folks in the extroverted, biased toward decisions, fiery side of whatever personality test you believe in tend to get the gist of this type of content. Folks who are more introverted or more conservative in their decision-making do not.

So if you're sitting there, a quiet person, a risk-averse person, a slow-to-act person, an introverted person, and you're saying, "This just doesn't apply to me," well, not so fast!

I once knew someone in consulting who was by far more introverted and less biased to action than me. For him, each client was a threat. They made what seemed to him to be unreasonable demands, they made them at unexpected hours of the day, and they provided unreasonable timelines for their demands. Now, his deeply held beliefs were different from mine. He believed that at work and in life in general, disaster was awaiting around every corner. And his knee-jerk reaction was, "Well, if disaster is waiting around each corner, best to eliminate all the corners." He was very *anti-change*. His stay-the-course mentality affected his whole life. Don't move, don't switch jobs, keep a routine, avoid new experiences, don't trust new people. For people like this consultant, knee-jerk reactions don't necessarily resemble the biased-toward-action, "loud" knee-jerks that I've personally exhibited in my life.

Instead, those knee-jerks can look more like this:

- Stopping to gather more data and more inputs from all parties

- Abdicating responsibility and escalating to a higher authority

- Saying "no" because an option is new and there's no institutional knowledge

- Saying "no" because we have too many things going on and need to focus

And on and on. These are conservative decisions often made *in response to change*, so you see them in business all the time. They look responsible and healthy. One might say they even look *wise*. Pumping brakes does seem wiser than lodging a brick on the gas pedal! And in some contexts they're the right decision. That said, most businesses are changing all the time, often healthily changing, and in response, I've seen folks, like my consulting acquaintance, make these conservative decisions emotionally and thoughtlessly, driven *by a fear of change*.

You see, it's easy to spot the anxiety-fueled rage machine in the room (hi, that's me), but what about the anxiety-fueled fear machine? Their decisions can often look safe and wise, but knee-jerk conservatism is still knee-jerk; a decision made without considering some options is still a lost opportunity.

We all have deeply held beliefs that boil down our complex reality to tropes, and we all have emotions that stem from those beliefs. Don't think this chapter doesn't apply to you just because your tendencies are quieter.

Enough with This Woo-Woo Feelings Stuff

I hope this chapter clicked with some of you. I know it feels like a tonal departure from what we've discussed so far, but that's because humans are *integrated beings*, and we need to address both the logical and emotional sides of us as leaders if we're going to make better decisions.

The whole deeply held belief thing may have struck you as too much "head shrinkage." That's OK. Here are the main points to take away from this chapter:

- Don't try to change your assumptions and feelings that cause knee-jerk reactions directly.

- Instead, adopt practices and recruit allies who can help you pause before a knee-jerk reaction.

- You will on occasion choose to go with a decision that's not your first inclination. After that decision has been executed, reflect on the results.

- Over time, the results of going with well-thought, rather than purely emotional, decisions will, via a reward-based feedback loop, change your underlying assumptions about the world and associated feelings. This will make it easier to make better decisions in the future.

I hope that's straightforward enough and not too woo-woo for you!

8

Shaping the Company for Success

Throughout this book we've talked about making decisions as something that takes place *in a context*. We could think about that as if we're trapped in a prison and told to escape. We have the tools that we have, and that's it. How do we get over or under those prison walls?

But that's not the right metaphor for our context at all!

Why? Because as leaders, *we shape our environment*. We control our context more than we know! A prison isn't a prison if the inmates can move the walls.

In this chapter, I want to focus on two things we can shape to make our decision-making processes more effective: **company culture** and **our people**.

Company Culture and Values

Over the years I've worked on a lot of packaging and pricing efforts. As I mentioned earlier in the book, I helped build pricing algorithms for Fortune 500s to make sure their products were priced most effectively to maximize their revenue. For me, then, pricing always felt like a tool for the company; you can price an airline ticket at $200 or at $400, and either price might be best for revenue depending on the dynamics of the market and competition.

One day, I had an interesting encounter with an employee on my team when it came to the topic of raising some prices. We were looking at a company's prices and noting that they hadn't been increased in a long time despite having competitor data showing us to be at the bottom of the market and having survey data that showed customers to be fairly insensitive to price changes.

My employee said to me with deep concern, "How do we justify raising prices? *This isn't customer-centric.*" It was an interesting point, albeit one that came as a surprise to me. After all, we were working for a for-profit company. The ultimate goal was indeed to grow the business and maximize revenue. And price was simply one tool for doing that; the current prices we'd be changing weren't free, so there was nothing sacred about them. I knew the previous dude who'd set the prices the last time, and he certainly wasn't trying to give the product away!

Keeping the customer at the heart of how they worked was a *value* of this company. After all, building products without understanding the needs of the customer (even if you don't exactly build them a "faster horse" as discussed in Chapter 2) is essential.

Given this company value, my employee was right, albeit in a simplistic way: any price increase is *anti-customer* at first glance. But only at first glance. After all, giving away the product for free would shut the company down, and then there'd be no products to sell! And nothing is less customer-friendly than offering them nothing.

I shrugged this comment off at first, but then I started noting similar rumblings from other employees across the company. Many folks felt the same way about price increases: price increases, in their opinion, were a violation of the company's customer-focused value. I was concerned.

What was going on? Why was I concerned?

Culture Is a Sum of Our Values, Explicit and Implicit

I'm going to give some homegrown definitions for some squishy words here. I'm not an anthropologist, a theologian, or in any way qualified to define these words. But I will nevertheless define them *through the lens of decision-making*.

What are values at a company? Well, we often know them as a list of statements printed on a company's career page, but what are they, really?

Values are beliefs that motivate choosing a particular option over another when making a decision.

If my company has a stated company value of "move fast and break things," this is a **decision-making shortcut** for the entire employee base. It communicates that when evaluating options, weigh the ones higher that bias toward rapid progress over the ones that tread carefully in an effort to not overturn the apple cart.

Why do people follow along with a stated company value? Well, they know it's *valued* by leadership, which means if leadership is to be trusted, then the value creates good outcomes for the business, and regardless of outcomes for the business, it is likely something the employee will be assessed on. Indeed, many companies bake their stated values into formal employee performance assessments.

Now, the example I just gave of a company value that's listed on the website or in the employee handbook, which is to say a value everyone can parrot back word for word, that's what I call an **explicit value**.

Alongside explicit values, companies (and just about any organization you can think of) accrue **implicit values** over time. An implicit value, like any other value, is a decision-making shortcut, but it's one that the company doesn't outright state in documents or teach employees. These values are *picked up* by new employees. They're "in the water supply" as they say.

While explicit values create behaviors, implicit values often arise as the sum of observed behaviors in the organization, which then gains a conscious or subconscious value status ("This is how we do things here") that then begets more of the same behavior.

For example, a company might have the following implicit value: "The early bird gets the worm." It's not stated in any of the company documents. It's not on the website. But the parking lot is full by 7 a.m. Any new employee is going to pick up on the behavior, and in their desire to fit in and to succeed, they are more likely than not to take up the behavior and adopt the implicit value. Creating implicit values can be as easy as the CEO or executive team doing something visible, which then gets emulated by the rest of the employee base (such as coming in early). Implicit values aren't necessarily bad, but as we'll discuss, they can take the company in odd directions when left unacknowledged and undealt with.

So, values then beget decisions (behaviors are, of course, decisions too), and those decisions can actually add more implicit behaviors to an organization, including changing or overriding the stated explicit values!

For example, a company might have a stated explicit value around ethical behavior. But if an employee joins the company and sees their colleagues engaging in unethical sales tactics and being rewarded for it, they might adopt an implicit value that actually overrides the explicit value.

OK, so those are values.

What's company culture?

Company culture consists of the shared, *held* values and resulting behaviors of the company. Culture is what you mean when you say "That's just how we do things." I emphasized the word "held," because a company can absolutely have explicit values that are stated but not actually held by anyone. All implicit values are held by definition; they're not written down anywhere, so the only way you know they exist is by observing people holding them.

Hypothetically, if Universal Studios has a value of "innovation" but then they release ten *Fast and the Furious* films (as of the publication of this book at least), one might argue that their explicit value is not actually held by the employees and therefore is not part of the culture. Meanwhile, they might not have an explicit value of "execute repetitive cash grabs," but employee behavior, exhibited in the content they produce, indicates this is an implicit value.

Good Leaders Actively Check On and Shape Their Culture to Produce Better Decisions

Culture then is the summation of a company's held values. It's a cheat sheet to how they make decisions more quickly. And every leader at a company engages in *shaping that culture*. By altering values, publishing them, behaving in ways that communicate implicit values, assessing performance based on values, speaking about values in town hall, etc., leaders shape the culture of a company and hence the decisions that company makes.

When I discovered that folks didn't want to raise prices, I was bumping up against the effects of a culture that had been *deliberately shaped* but with rather poor execution. Folks knew they needed to be customer centric, they'd heard it time and again in company communications, but what that meant hadn't been defined well in terms of the end goal: understand and serve customers so they'll want to buy more from us and stay with us longer because our products meet their needs. The value had been preached in a vague enough way to permit an us-versus-them mentality in the company where customers were the good guys, and the company itself was a bad guy for attempting to increase revenue.

Shaping culture *well* then becomes a skill for ensuring good decisions aren't just made by the leader themselves but by all those under them. So many decisions are made by folks under a leader rather than by the leader themselves. Micro-managing folks isn't scalable as a means of making sure that everyone is making decisions in line with how a leader might. So, shaping culture, i.e., value-setting and communication, offers us a tool (albeit a coarse one) for scaling what "good decision-making" looks like according to that company's leadership. If moving fast is important for a leader, they can enshrine it in the company's culture. If coming to work early is important for a leader, they can enshrine that too.

To shape culture well means not only to define a value but to provide examples of that value when it's executed well and when it's executed poorly; you must go beyond stating the value and get into interpreting it for folks time and again until the boots on the ground interpret it in a context when evaluating options just as you might.

And this is not a "once and done" activity. **Great leaders check on the behaviors their values are creating regularly**. Why? Well, the context of a business is always shifting. The market changes, competition changes, the expectations of a product changes, material costs change, you name it. And that means that decision-making changes! Our priorities and options shift. If that's the case, then our values and culture, which are tools for consistent decision-making across the company, might also *have to change*. Company values are not the 10 Commandments; change them to suit the decision-making needs of the company.

For example, if your values as a company include "move fast and break things" and then you, say, destabilize global democracy (ahem) and invite regulation as a result of this value, it might be time to acknowledge the world has changed a bit and swap out that value for another one.

In this way, I'm advocating for (harkening back to the introduction of this book) company value *relativism*. You don't get to canonize your values and throw up your hands and say, "This is how we must act in every situation." No, if being a "wise" leader means making good decisions contextually, then you are responsible for any tool you mint at the company for making good decisions, and that includes your company values. If they result in bad decisions, change them!

Now, I said culture-shaping is a "*coarse*" tool, because as I've argued repeatedly in this book, good decisions take into account their full context, whereas culture creates a *contextless set of shortcuts for making decisions*. That's what values do! They communicate, "Regardless of the situation, act this way." So, that streamlines things, and it gives the leader a little predictability below them. But there are costs to be aware of. Let's discuss them.

Culture Eats Decision-Making for Breakfast

Peter Drucker famously said, "Culture eats strategy for breakfast." In the context of this book, I'll make that more concrete: culture eats your decision-making for breakfast. Since culture is the lived-out summation of a company's held values, it's the "shortcut stew" of decision-making (and often decision *unmaking*).

Let's then list the ways in which culture impacts the decision-making process laid out in this book.

- **Culture shapes priorities:** As discussed in Chapter 4, a problem needs to be framed in terms of the one priority that must be addressed. Is it lowering costs? Is it increasing your growth rate? Culture tips the priority scales oftentimes, and we need to be aware that it can sometimes tip it in the wrong direction. If a business, say Costco, has a value of keeping costs and prices low, then that value, which is engrained in the culture, will shift the priority of many decisions over to keeping costs low. It's safe, it's a value held by your boss, etc.

- **Culture shapes option generation:** To the extent that we consult those internally at our company only to generate options for solving a problem, we're likely to generate options mostly in line with our culture. Picking up the Costco example again, if I were in leadership there and sourcing options for solving a problem from employees and colleagues, it would be unlikely that I'd source many options resulting in a price increase of the hotdogs and pizza at the front of the store.

- **Culture shapes option selection:** Since culture shapes the set of options considered and the priority by which they're sorted, culture shapes what we choose!

- **Culture shapes our vetting processes:** Let's say we run a premortem on a decision and we invite colleagues who all share the same values and are immersed in the same company culture. All their critiques are likely to be in line with company values. This means that in a premortem you're unlikely to get someone saying, "Are you sure we shouldn't just increase the price of the Costco hotdog?"

In other words, company culture impacts *every* step of the decision-making process. This can streamline things and make you go faster. That's OK for decisions of lesser importance sometimes (although I still like to test the electric fences of culture at least in my own thought processes even on quick decisions), but for the big decisions, the company-shifting ones, we need to remain aware of the *company cultural biases* present at every stage in our decision-making.

So How Do We Eat Culture for Breakfast?

How do we eat culture for breakfast? Easy! Yogurt! As a father of three children, I reserve the right to make one yogurt culture joke every few months.

It's important to acknowledge that a company's values and the accumulated culture that shape its decision-making processes isn't necessarily bad. Costco *wants to keep prices low*, so it's likely OK that every aspect of the decision-making process is shaped by this value. They want their values in the water supply as it were. That can be really good leadership because it scales good decision-making!

Where things get bad, though, is when **culture is unintentionally and without acknowledgment shaping your decisions.** This discussion should feel very similar to Chapter 7's discussion of emotions. In a way, culture is like the company's emotional compass that it overlays on each employee, shaping their own knee-jerk decision-making makeup.

"We don't raise prices, because that's not customer centric," is a knee-jerk cultural reaction, in this case based on an explicit value at the company I was working with. The reaction was used to obviate the option to raise prices almost as soon as it was proposed. At least in my example, the employee at least cited the value, however inappropriately. It's even scarier when the value is unstated and often unrealized!

How do we put this in check? It's as simple as *remaining conscious* of our values, associated cultural biases, and the ways they shape each aspect of our company's decision-making. Let's go back through the previous list:

- **Culture shapes priorities:** Pay mind in your own thinking and in conversation with colleagues as to whether your priority in solving a problem is driven by your culture and values. It's OK if it is; after all, your values are your values for a reason. But take a moment to check whether you're being influenced in this way and whether it's appropriate.

  Taking my example of customer-centricity a little further, that conversation with myself or with a colleague might have included something like, "Yes, customer centricity is a value. The priority in pricing, however, over the long term is revenue maximization. That said, we acknowledge that long term customer-unfriendly pricing will diminish net dollar retention, so we seek to maximize revenue in a sustainable way that does not spike churn or competitive threats as measures of customer unhappiness."

  To use the words of Chapter 4, I just made customer centricity a constraint (limiting churn) rather than an objective (maximizing revenue).

- **Culture shapes option generation:** In Chapter 3, I recommend that you pursue resources inside and outside the company to generate options. In a company with a very unified and strong set of values, sourcing all your options from inside its walls can lead to a rather one-sided set of options.

  Growing up I had a friend named Johnny who ate pizza *every day* for dinner. It was honestly pretty wild how little his parents cared about the amount of pizza he took in. Whenever I asked him what he wanted to eat, I knew what his answer would be: pizza. He ended up dropping a hot slice of cheese on his thigh and got a pretty bad burn; I thought this would change his love for the pie, but it didn't. He and pizza were going the distance.

That's what it can feel like to source options at a company with a strong culture. Every option is pizza even if it's going to burn your thighs.

Therefore, *going outside the company*, whether that's to your professional network, to business books, to metaphorically related media is an important tactic for avoiding being solely culturally influenced when generating options for solving a problem. Additionally, if you end up swimming in options generated internally, don't forget to pull a "10th man" on them like we discussed in Chapter 3; purposefully explore the opposite paths to these culturally homogenous options.

One more thought! It's important to remember that it takes new employees some amount of time before they become indoctrinated by company culture, so purposefully targeting new hires (even if you have to pull ideas from folks further down the career ladder) in discussions of how a problem might be solved can be helpful. Tenure is an under-leveraged thought diversity vector at many companies, where the "new guy" (or gal) is often actively *ignored* rather than used because they haven't been brainwashed yet.

- **Culture shapes option selection:** In Chapter 3, we discussed listing and even charting the options we might take; in a similar vein, we can label which options are in keeping with company values and which are not. An option that is not in keeping with company values may be dismissed immediately or not depending on how sacrosanct the value.

If you have a value that says "Do no evil" and you have an option that's evil, well, that might be worth dismissing out of hand. If you have a value that says, "Move fast and break things," but you have an option that says, "Take the time to retool the product to comply with European data privacy laws," well, that may be worth keeping around even though it's a violation of the value at first glance. Sigh...European Union laws are the pits. I digress.

With your options labeled, you'll be able to acknowledge the ways in which company culture aligns with each option and choose explicitly how much credit to give options that stay in line with your values. Remember, we're not looking to purge company culture from the decision; we just want to make that bias *conscious* rather than unconscious.

- **Culture shapes our vetting processes:** When it comes time then to "sit with" the decision you're making, once again, just keep company culture front of mind when pulling data or executing a premortem. Of course, someone will critique a decision according to company values if it runs afoul of them. Of course, data is likely to be interpreted in line with company values. Simply acknowledging this in the room when a discussion is taking place, making the bias one that's consciously stated for the group, can help calibrate how to modify or backtrack on a decision if it's not in line with culture. Similarly, by acknowledging company culture, you can stay on the lookout for a bunch of "yes men" style of agreement with a decision merely because it's in line with values. If the company value is "Move fast and break things," and the premortem is just a bunch of folks shouting, "Let's go!" then you may want to acknowledge the bias in the room and ask pointed questions *against the grain of the company values* to spur more productive discussion.

Making Implicit Values Explicit

Everything discussed can be helpful when the culture you're making decisions in is driven by explicit values. But so often our company cultures are driven by implicit, i.e., unstated, values even more than explicit ones. These are like unacknowledged "deeply held beliefs" from Chapter 7. These values create knee-jerk reactions to potential decisions without folks ever acknowledging the shared implicit value driving their behavior.

The first step in managing implicit values and the way they impact your decision-making is by identifying them; i.e., the first step is "admitting you have a problem" as they say.

Sometimes these implicit values are as easy to identify as taking a beat and asking yourself, "What are the ways 'we do business here,' i.e., common behaviors and beliefs that are shared by employees at the company, which **are not** part of our explicit values?"

That's a good conversation to have with yourself. Seriously. Give it a shot now.

That said, if you want to get serious about this, I encourage you as a leader to execute the following exercise, ideally with others at the company, including cross-functional leaders and perhaps even HR.

The exercise is simple: first, **go through the company's explicit values and discuss what each of them means.** Is there a generally agreed-on interpretation of each value and its practical applications? If yes, great! If not, then you might have your first implicit value problem. Why? Because implicit values can often stem from misinterpretations of vague or poorly explained explicit values, which then take on a life of their own.

Are there common misinterpretations of your explicit values leading to other implicit ones?

In my pricing example, there was an explicit value of "customer-centricity," but its misinterpretation and misapplication led to an implicit value of "charging more money for products is wrong."

All right, so catalog those common misinterpretations. Schedule time to clarify these explicit values with company leadership and communicate the clarifications *broadly and repeatedly* in order to change your culture.

Such a clarification for my customer-centricity situation might mean repeated communication to the employees about *how we live out customer-centricity through great customer support, excellent customer research in R&D, and a well-designed and documented product that meets our customers' needs*. Basically, we can use positive examples of the value lived out to communicate better what the value means.

Now, moving on with our exercise, you should next ask some variation of the following questions: What values do we all hold here that aren't explained by our explicit values or their misinterpretations? What decisions do we tend to make over and over again that don't hang logically off the values we have written down (even their misinterpretation)?

List any such tendencies and try to boil down what's going on *into value statements*. These tendencies are then reverse engineered into explicit value *candidates*, more or less.

As an example, perhaps you notice that everyone comes in early to work, let's say between 7 a.m. and 8 a.m. You ask the room why folks do it. Well, it's just how we do things here. OK, that sounds like an implicit value phenomenon. The explicit value candidate might then be "The early bird gets the worm."

Once you've got these implicit values stated, then you need to ask the question, "Should any of these values be made explicit?"

If yes, make them explicit to clear up confusion and take control of the company culture.

If no, well, then there's a problem! You've got a company value that people are acting on that you're uncomfortable making explicit. What are you going to do about that?

The answer could be doing nothing if the value is innocuous enough (folks come in early every day, and while we're fine with that, we don't want to enshrine that in writing). Perhaps you decide to take a single step beyond doing nothing and merely remind employees it's not a value.

That's easy enough. Communication could go something like, "Hey, folks! We know a lot of you come in early. And that's awesome if you wanna get that 'early worm.' Just know that work hours are a little more flexible than that, and we only expect everyone to be online for the shared work hours of 9 a.m. to 5 p.m. EST, and whether you get in the rest of your workweek after those hours or before those hours, well, that's up to you, especially if you're remote in a different time zone."

For some implicit values, ignoring them or clarifying them may not be enough. You may need to get the company to **repudiate them**, especially if they've got lots of *momentum* that's leading to bad decision-making at the company repeatedly. This means first explicitly stating the value and behaviors you find are being held at the company (perhaps even by leadership) that are unproductive and then providing folks with reasons why that value is not congruent with the company's explicit values and culture it's seeking to create.

Let's take the example of a company that thrives on "doing things that don't scale" even though that value isn't explicitly stated anywhere. They solve each problem using massive amounts of manpower, and oftentimes they don't invest in making these investments efficient later.

What might you say to repudiate such behavior? It might go like this:

"Hey y'all! We always lean into 'doing things that don't scale' in every decision we make. We throw bodies at every problem, and if a problem can't be solved with manpower, then we don't solve that problem at all. Well, this way of doing business just isn't working for us. Maybe it worked for us in the past, but it's not working now!"

At this point, you'd insert some examples perhaps before continuing. . .

"Note that this way of working isn't one of our values, and it's occasionally getting us in trouble. Now I'm not saying we should *never* act this way. Sometimes we absolutely *should* do things that don't scale and test processes with lots of people power before we systemize things. But let's be careful and not get ourselves bogged down with tons of human investments and very little systems longer than we intend to. Let's enter into these decisions with our eyes wide open for opportunities to scale using tools other than people power."

Does a little communication like this fix the problem? Probably not! But it's a start. The best way to change implicit values is to make comments like that **over and over again** every time you see folks acting out of the implicit value *unthinkingly*. You've got to create a habit of making the implicit value conscious until people recognize it themselves and remember that it's not necessarily "how we do things." And most importantly, you as a leader need to model the alternative behavior you're looking to encourage.

This is a real investment in energy. Changing momentum is often harder than getting something moving from a dead stop.

OK, so that's how values and culture affect making great decisions. While you're endeavoring to create a company culture derived from explicit values that helpfully shortcut the decision-making process for your company's context, remember that that's the long game, and in the meantime, you can always keep company cultural effects in mind while evaluating options. That's fast and costs you nothing.

People: Hiring, Managing, Promoting, and Firing

Manipulating values and culture is an excellent way for a leader to scale decision-making practices at a company. There's another tool leaders have at their disposal as well: controlling who's at the company! Indeed, hiring great decision-makers, promoting great decision-makers into roles of greater authority, and moving poor decision-makers out of authority or out of the company constitute some of the best uses of a leader's time in making sure that great decisions are made at their company.

This isn't a book on hiring and managing people, but I want to spend some time bringing these activities in line with the practices in this book.

Hire People Who've Read and Like This Book

I'm kidding! That'd probably lead to you merely hiring my mother.

That said, the processes in Chapters 3 and 4 that constitute how good decisions are made isn't rocket science. I encounter candidates *all the time* who intuitively or even intentionally make decisions in ways similar to what I've detailed in this book.

To screen for folks like that, I recommend asking questions in a few areas during candidate interviews. I'll list them for you:

1. **Can state problems clearly:** "Name an important problem you had to solve in a past role where you had to make an important decision."

2. **Can identify priorities and constraints well:** "What was your main priority in making this decision? Were there other concerns you had to juggle alongside that priority? How'd you handle that?"

3. **Can identify options well:** "What were some options to solve that problem?"

4. **Can articulate prioritization well:** "Why did you ultimately decide the way you did?"

5. **Can they kick the tires on a decision well:** "How did you sanity check your decision?"

6. **Can they maximize the probability of success of a decision:** "What did you do to ensure success?"

7. **Probe on collaboration:** "In generating the possible ways to make that decision or in kicking the tires on your decision or in any other step of the way, how did you leverage the folks around you (whatever that means to you) to make sure you were making a good decision?"

8. **Can they learn from their decisions:** "How did things ultimately turn out? What'd you learn? Would you do things the same way next time?"

If practiced enough, these questions can come of as conversational and a lot less formal. During the conversation, if you find an opening, you can probe on their emotional self-awareness. Depending on the role, you can ask further questions on data analysis or specific constraint considerations (resources, budget, etc.).

I'll be honest, I have a low view of interviewing candidates in general. Making good decisions repeatedly over time is *very different* from interviewing well. I've seen far too many candidates who impress in interviews only to totally fail in practice (because leadership is contextual and their past context won't be the same as their future context!) to think that interviews are a panacea for hiring.

But the previous questions can screen out folks who have trouble articulating why they do what they do, who defer or escalate important decisions to others, who lean overly much on how companies "just do business," who can't determine what's a priority and what's a constraint, etc.

Give Less Responsibility to Those Who Make Poor Decisions. Give More to Those Who Make Great Decisions

Promoting and firing are two sides of the same coin.

If you've got an employee who makes bad decisions, who doesn't make fully loaded decisions, who doesn't commit to their decisions and self-sabotages, who doesn't look for off-ramps and two-way doors, who doesn't "use all the parts of the animal," who doesn't take the time (this can quite literally mean clocking enough time) to do the work of making good decisions, then you've got a problem. **Bad decision-makers need to be removed from making important decisions as quickly as possible.** I hope that doesn't come off as too callus; leadership affects company outcomes and other people too much to leave folks in roles that have ripple effects.

When it comes then to managing an organization that emphasizes good decision-making from top to bottom, here are three tips you should remember:

- **"Hope is not a strategy"**: Don't hope an employee will start making better decisions. If they're not good at doing what the company needs them to do, cut them fast. Avoiding making this call and just "seeing how things pan out" is often a bad decision (use the process in this book to get intentional about deciding whether to keep someone). If you agree with me that interviewing as a tool is rather inaccurate, then firing fast is a great remedy. If getting someone valuable involves an element of chance, then you need to flip that coin as many times as you can to have it come up heads! Increase the throughput of trying folks out in the context of your company and team in order to make sure you have the right people.

- **Hold people accountable for their decision-making above all else:** In so many of my performance conversations with folks, they focus on a couple of things: how hard they've worked and how long they've been with the company. Curiously enough, it's often the folks who've gotten straight A's and always succeeded in life that appeal to tenure and hard work; maybe they're just used to trophies and diplomas coming to them at regular intervals, and they believe companies should operate that way too!

  Hard work and tenure do not make a great leader. I could work exceptionally hard at becoming a great guitarist. I could work at it for a long time. Both of those *increase the probability of me being good at guitar*. But ultimately folks will assess my abilities based on how well I play. The same goes for leadership in business. Experience (of which tenure is a component) and hard work increase someone's odds of being a good decision-maker. But it's best to hold people accountable to whether they're following practices like those listed in this book.

  Now, holding someone accountable for being a good decision-maker *does not mean that their decisions are always successful*. Merely assessing folks based on *not failing* will lead to a lack of risk taking in your organization. Instead, assess folks on how they arrive at their decisions, communicate and execute their decisions, and learn and iterate from their decisions. If you assess these strengths rather than successful outcomes directly, oddly, you'll increase the success of your organization, because you'll get solid decision-making processes combined with a well-moderated fear of failure.

- **Spend your time on your best leaders, not coaching your underperformers:** You'll get more impact by spending time with and coaching your highest performers under you. Good decision-makers under you exponentially increase your own positive impact. So often you will be encouraged (I've spent a lot of time with HR duking it out on this point) to spend your time coaching up your worst performers. Getting a C player up to a B won't get you as much impact as taking an A player to an A+. So invest in the A players and cut those who struggle faster than your compunction might lead you to.

Some of these tips aren't going to make you many friends, I'll admit. So many of us are wired to bring up the performance of our weakest players to match that of our strongest, which is often impossible, and which robs the strong performers of the attention they deserve. Remember, nothing here needs to be done heartlessly. If you make expectations clear, if you keep track of decision-making responsibilities and performance, and if you transparently take people through how they're doing, folks often know whether something is working out or not before you have the hard conversation with them. And someone who's struggling to make great decisions in one job might be masterful in another. So much of this book is arguing that business is complex and highly contextual; the same applies to folks' performance. They can be excellent in one role and then fail miserably in another. Being honest with them and moving them on to something else can be a gift.

All that said, while leaders in one role may fail while they used to be successful elsewhere, by applying the elements of this book, I believe that that inconsistency can be *vastly reduced* because it's often gut-based decision-making, not intentional "wise" decision-making, which can vary so much depending on context.

Scale Your Impact

Up to this chapter, we dived deep into how you as a leader can make great decisions. And understanding your company's culture and surrounding yourself with great folks helps with that! However, this chapter is different than the previous ones in that we've gotten into how you can *tailor the environment at your company to make sure everyone makes great decisions.*

Be intentional about how you set, communicate, and clarify the values that shape company culture.

Be intentional in who you hire, who you fire, and who you coach up.

These are ways of scaling your impact beyond the reach of your own decisions.

Conclusion

That's what I've got! Let me distill it down for you from the intro to the end:

- **Make good decisions to be a good leader:** Leadership is all about making good decisions repeatedly over time.

- **Be wise:** Business decisions are highly complex and highly contextual. Often polar opposite options for solving a problem can seem attractive, and both options may have all kinds of advocacy, including various business books, backing them up. We see these contradictory options in all areas of business whether we're considering people, processes, or products. Choosing between good options contextually is what makes a leader *wise*, which is what this book is about.

  - **We flee to simplicity because it's comfortable:** There is no way to boil down good decision-making to a set of aphorisms that succeed in all settings. This is why so many business books have a shelf life of a month until you read the next business book. They present one way of going about things as if it's the only way when our experience would tell us otherwise. We actually flee to business books and gurus, because their certitude is more comfortable than operating contextually.

- **Define your priority and source many options:** We can make better decisions when we acknowledge contextuality, define our problem and priority well, and source many options for solving the problem *employing the space of possible levers we might pull as a leader and as a company.* From these options, based on our single priority and any associated constraints, we need to rank and choose what's best.
  - **Source options from all over the place:** Options for solving a problem can come from those closest to the problem, those far away in your professional network, or even from fictional characters in a Disney movie. Sourcing options from a variety of sources in and outside the company will maximize your chances of landing on something great.
  - **You get only one priority:** When sorting options for solving your problem, you must have only one priority. If you've got two, you're not likely to choose the best answer. Turn secondary priorities into constraints.
- **Bias toward learning, iteration, and two-way doors:** When sorting options, it's best to give weight to those options that allow us to learn and iterate quickly or which provide "two-way doors."
- **Pull the data, sit with the decision:** For important decisions, slow down and pull additional data either qualitative or quantitative. Role-play a decision's failure ahead of time via a premortem.
- **Execution is *not* a distinct phase after decision-making:** Consider your options "fully loaded," i.e., with attention given to operational and execution concerns from the get-go.
- **Know when to hold 'em and when to fold 'em:** Establish success and failure criteria up front when making a decision so you know whether it's failed or succeeded as soon as can

be determined. This will allow you to take the nearest off-ramp or to adjust in flight.

- **Good leaders intentionally work on their own emotional maturity:** A good decision-making process requires that we *get out of our own way* when making decisions. Our emotional knee-jerk reactions, while an excellent source for generating options, will attempt to shortcut our decision-making and lead to suboptimal outcomes. We can use meditative practices, counselors, and allies to reshape these knee-jerk tendencies through positive feedback loops.

- **Be transparent:** Having made a decision, be transparent with those needed to execute the decision and those who are affected. It helps unify around a common goal, builds trust, and lets folks understand their part of the whole.

- **Commit to the bit:** Commit to a decision even if you know the odds of failure are substantial and even though you're keeping your eyes open for off-ramps. Modeling commitment ensures the best effort from you and from those paying attention to your behavior.

- **Use all the parts of the animal:** Use all the tools the company provides for you to succeed in your decisions from sales and marketing to engineering to HR and finance.

- **Be aware of your company's culture. Shape it to succeed:** We make decisions inside the context of our company, complete with its culture and values. You can shape that culture to help allow for better decision-making.

- **Create a team of great decision-makers:** Hire employees and hold them accountable to the behaviors and processes in this book. This will scale your leadership effectiveness beyond the decisions you make personally to those made by your direct reports and colleagues.

Wow, that's actually more bullets than I thought I was going to have when I started writing this section.

I want to be honest though. When I wrote that list, I didn't think to myself, "Yep, got it, yep, yep, doing that super well, that too, mhmm. . . ." No, I'm humbled. Moreover, I'm embarrassed. I fail on any number of those bullets weekly.

I didn't write this book because I feel I embody these ideas well all the time. Sometimes I do well. Sometimes I regress.

At the height of my panic disorder, I started going to a counselor weekly. And he described the process of recovery to me, which is to say the process of changing the behaviors that were feeding my panic, as a journey that would **improve on average** year after year. In fact, **I might have the occasional regression from month to month or week to week.**

Becoming a better leader is much the same. We're humans; our progress toward becoming better at anything is rarely linear. Occasionally I burn the hamburgers, I injure my back, I yell at my kids. Remember, a batting average above .400 is considered a phenomenal achievement for a professional baseball player, and business is far more complex than batting (easy for me to say. . . I don't play baseball).

With these ideas, the thing I have to remind myself is that each day I choose again to *practice* good decision-making. My failures, while they make me feel hypocritical, needn't prevent me from dusting myself off and trying to make that next leadership decision as best I can. And my progress is on average in the right direction, although I have periods where I personally regress into a knee-jerk control freak. I hope you'll take the same long view; you're looking for progress over perfection. Like Truman Capote said, "Failure is the condiment that gives success its flavor." I live in Utah where that condiment is a mixture of ketchup and mayonnaise. I can think of nothing better!

Well, I hope you've enjoyed this discussion. I'll leave you here at the end with some *options*: feel free to reach out to me on Twitter at (@John4man), follow me on LinkedIn (John Foreman), or email me with feedback (John.4man@gmail.com). Weigh your decision carefully! And I wish you wisdom in all your future endeavors.

Acknowledgments

Many thanks to Eric Rea, Ben Chestnut, Farrah Kennedy, and the many others who've extended me opportunities to lead and to learn. Thanks also to all those I've led, often poorly, for their forbearance.

I'd also like to give a special thanks to Pauline Reader for her complete denial that I could string enough words together coherently to write a book. This one's for you, Pauline!

About the Author

John W. Foreman is the chief product officer for Podium, a Google Ventures and Y Combinator–backed tech startup that's reshaping how local businesses operate and grow. Prior to Podium, John Foreman was chief product officer of Mailchimp, which ultimately sold to Intuit for $12 billion. John has built software to help millions of businesses succeed for more than a decade.

While John's work is in leading R&D for tech companies, his background is in data science and artificial intelligence. His first book, *Data Smart: Using Data Science to Transform Information into Insight*, helped professionals around the world learn how to apply artificial intelligence techniques in their own fields.

John lives in Salt Lake City, Utah, with his wife Lydia, his three sons, and his two troublesome dogs. The corgi, in particular, needs an attitude adjustment. John loves deep frying things, and he's a terrible driver.

Index